ESL Vocabulary and Idioms

Volume 2 – Intermediate and Advanced Levels

Elizabeth Gamburd

The chapters presented in this book are based on classroom handouts. Since it is impossible to cover all English words and phrases, the lessons are representative of the covered categories.

TABLE OF CONTENTS

ANTONYMS

Intermediate Level Antonyms

Absent/present	Fancy/plain	Part/whole	Ugly/beautiful
Against/for	Finish/begin	Patient/impatient	Uncertain/certain
Beneath/above	Floor/ceiling	Polite/rude	Wake/sleep
Bitter/sweet	Foolish/wise	Question/answer	War/peace
Borrow/lend	Forget/remember	Quick/slow	Warm/cool
Brave/scared	Forward/backward	Reward/punishment	Whisper/yell
Buy/sell	Gather/scatter	Rough/smooth	Whole/part
Careful/careless	Glad/sorry	Selfish/unselfish	Wide/narrow
Cheerful/sad	Graceful/clumsy	Sell/buy	Winter/ Summer
Complete/incomplete	Guilty/innocent	Send/receive	
Crooked/straight	Hide/show	Sharp/dull	
Cruel/kind	Increase/decrease	Silent/loud	
Death/life	Intelligent/stupid	Sink/float	
Deep/shallow	Lead/follow	Smart/stupid	
Different/same	Length/width	Stay/go	
Double/single	Mean/pleasant	Stranger/acquaintance	
East/west	Loose/tight	Strong/weak	
Enemy/friend	Lose/find	Sweet/sour	
Exciting/dull	Lower/raise	Tame/wild	
Exit/entrance	North/south	Thin/thick	
Expensive/cheap	Often/seldom	Thin/fat	
Fail/succeed	Outer/inner	True/false	

QUESTIONS FOR ORAL DISCUSSION OR HOMEWORK

1. Which antonyms are used for directions?

2. Which antonyms do we use for weather and seasons?

3. Which antonyms are also prepositions of place?

4. Which antonyms do you like the sound of?

   Which antonyms do dislike?

5. How are antonyms used in your language?

Advanced Level Antonyms

Abundant/scarce
Accept/refuse
Accidental/intentional
Accurate/incorrect
Admit/deny
Advance/retreat
Antique/modern
Attack/defend
Authentic/imitation
Beg/offer
Cease/begin
Combine/separate
Comedy/tragedy
Condemn/praise
Completely/partly
Conquer/fail
Contract/expand
Dangerous/safe
Depart/arrive
Destroy/create
Discourage/encourage
Disgrace/honor
Dwarf/overshadow
Ebb/flood
Evil/good
Exhibit/conceal
Exterior/interior
Extinguish/ignite
Famous/unknown
Fertile/barren
Fiction/fact
Former/latter
Frequent/infrequent

Generous/miserly
Genuine/fake
Grin/frown
Harmony/discord
Harsh/mild
Humble/proud
Idle/busy
Illegal/lawful
Imaginary/real
Import/export
Imprison/free
Include/exclude
Inferior/superior
Joy/grief
Knowledge/ignorance
Lazy/industrious
Literal/figurative
Majority/minority
Maximum/minimum
Merciful/cruel
Miserable/happy
Mix/sort
Moisture/dryness
Naked/clothed
Necessary/useless
Nourish/starve
Obey/disobey
Outer/inner
Perfect/imperfect
Permit/forbid
Pro/com
Positive/negative
Private/public

Prohibit/allow
Reluctant/enthusiastic
Sane/insane
Shrink/expand
Simple/complicated
Slavery/freedom
Solid/liquid
Spend/save
Stationary/moveable
Stiff/limp
Strengthen/weaken
Surrender/continue
Swift/slow
Tangible/intangible
Tardy/early
Temporary/permanent
Thaw/freeze
Tough/tender
Tough/weak
Triumph/fail
Unbreakable/fragile
Unique/ordinary
Useful/useless
Usually/rarely
Vacant/occupied
Vanish/appear
Victory/defeat
Villain/hero
Violent/gentle
Wealthy/poor
Worthless/valuable

QUESTIONS FOR ORAL DISCUSSION OR HOMEWORK

1. Why does English have so many different antonyms?

2. Which languages have contributed antonyms to the English language?

3. Which of the advanced antonyms do you like? Dislike?

4. Are these antonyms more difficult for you to use?

   Why?

ASTRONOMY AND GEOGRAPHY

Astronomy

Space

- Asteroid
  Black hole
  Comet
- Constellation
- Falling star
  Galaxy
- Meteor
- Meteor shower

- Meteorite
  Moon
- Nebula
  Orbit
  Outer space
  Planet
- Planetoid
  Ring

  Satellite
  Shooting star
- Solar wind
  Space
  Star
  Sun
- Sun spots
  Universe

Solar System

- Asteroid belt
  Earth (3)
  Jupiter (5)
  Mars (4)

  Mercury (1)
  Moons
  Neptune (8)
  Pluto (9)***

  Saturn (6)
  Sun
  Uranus (7)
  Venus (2)

*Number in parentheses denotes position from the Sun
***Pluto has be downgraded to a moon and is no longer considered a planet.

Earth Geography

Latitude
Antarctic Circle
Arctic Circle
Equator
Tropic of Cancer
Tropic of Capricorn

Directions
East/Southeast/Northeast
North
South
West/Southwest/Northwest

Area	Crater	Gorge	North Pole	South Pole
Atoll	Current	Gulf	Ocean	Strait
Bay	Dale	Gully	Peak	Stream
Beach	Dam	Hill	Peninsula	Surf
Bog	Delta	Iceberg	Plain	Swamp
Brook	Desert	Island	Plateau	Tide
Canal	Ditch	Isthmus	Pond	Undertow
Canyon	Estuary	Lagoon	Prairie	Valley
Cape	Fault	Lake	Range	Volcano
Cascade	Field	Latitude	Ravine	Waterfall
Channel	Fiord	Ledge	Reef	Wave
Chasm	Forest	Longitude	Reservoir	Woods
Cliff	Geyser	Marsh	Rift	Caldera
Coastline	Glacier	Meadow	River	
Continent	Globe	Mountain	Sea	

Earth's Oceans, Rivers and Major Lakes

Oceans
Atlantic
S.Atlantic
Artic
Baltic Sea
Barents Sea
Black Sea
East China Sea
Indian
Pacific
S. Pacific
Aral

Philippine Sea
Tasmanian Sea
Mediterranean Sea
Aegean Sea
Red Sea
Bering Sea
Greenland Sea
Norway Sea
Caspian Sea
North Sea
Caribbean
Gulf of Mexico

Irish Sea
Sea of Okhotsk
RIVERS:
Nile River
Amazon
Yangtze
Mississippi
Yenisey-Angara
Huang-Ho
Ob'Irtysh
Rio Parana
Amur-Shilka

Lena
Congo
Mekong
Niger

Lakes
Baikal
Titicaca
Michigan
Superior
Huron

Materials

Dirt	Mud	Stone
Earth	Pebble	Turf
Grass/sod	Rock	Fresh Water
Lava	Soil	Salt Water

Natural Events

Aftershock	Erosion	Hurricane	Tsunami
Avalanche	Eruption	Landslide	Typhoon
Earthquake	Flood	Tidal wave	Water spout
Ebb	Flow	Tornado/cyclone	Whirlpool

Adjectives

Alluvial	Fertile	Remote
Arid	Forested	Semi-arid
Artic	Hilly	Semi-tropical
Barren	Mediterranean	Southern
Central	Mountainous	Tropical
Coastal	Northern	Tundra
Desert	Outback	Western
Drought prone	Peninsular	Wet
Eastern	Plains	Wooded

Idioms

A stick in the mud	Leave no stone unturned	Spaced out
Babes in the woods	Left high and dry	Still waters run deep
Bog down with	Make a mountain out of a molehill	Test the water
Can't see the forest for the trees	Make waves	Tip of the iceberg
Dirt cheap	Move mountains	Under the sun
Down-to-earth	Once in a blue moon	Under the weather
East is east and West is west	Out of the woods	Watch the world go by
have stars in your eyes	Out of this world	Watch this space
In hot water	Over the hill	Win by a landslide
It's a small world	Reach for the stars	World is your oyster

QUESTIONS FOR DISCUSSION OR HOMEWORK

1. What type of country do you come from?

2. What are the various regions of your country?

3. Describe the various regions of the United States.

4. If you could visit another planet in the solar system, which planet would you like to visit?

5. Why this particular planet?

6. Which oceans and rivers have you swum in?

7. What is the difference between and ocean and a sea?

8. A lake and pond?

    A mountain and a hill?

BANKS, MONEY AND CREDIT

Nouns

401(k)	Credit account	Money	Withdrawal slip
Asset	Credit card	Mortgage	Withdrawal
ATM-automatic teller machine	Credit history	Nickel	
Automatic payment	Currency	Paycheck	
Balance	Debit card	Penalty	
Bank account	Deposit	Penny	
Bank book	Deposit slip	Piggy bank	
Bankruptcy	Dime	Principal	
Bank	Dollar	Quarter	
Bill	Due date	Receipt	
Billing date	Frozen assets	Record book	
Buck	Half dollar	Safe	
Cash	Inheritance	Safety deposit box	
CD-certificate of deposit	INS- insufficient funds	Savings account	
Charge account	Interest	Second mortgage	
Check	Interest rate	Secured loan	
Check book	Invoice	Statement	
Check register	IRA	Total	
Check stub	Line of credit	Traveler's check	
Checking account	Loan	VAT- value added tax	
Coin	Loan agreement	Vault	
Commercial loan	Loan payment	Window	

Verbs

Alleviate	Convert	Make change
Apply for	Count	Overdraw
Authorize	Credit	Overdrawn
Balance	Debit	Pay
Borrow	Deposit	Put in
Budget	Endorse	Repay
Cancel	Expire	Save
Cancel	Incur	Stop payment
Cash	Insure	Take out
Change	Justify	Transfer
Charge	Loan	Withdraw
Close out	Lend	

Bank Personnel

Drive- up teller	President	Teller
Executive officer	Safe deposit clerk	
Fraud officer	Secretary	
Loan officer	Security guard	

Idioms

A man of means	Don't bank on that	Pass the buck
Ante up	Easy money	Pay back
Bank holiday	Flat broke	Pick up the tab
Bank on something	Funny money	Pinch pennies
Be a steal	Have money to burn	Pretty penny
Be broke	I.O.U.	Put aside
Be on a budget	In the money	Queer as a three-dollar bill
Bottom dollar	Layaway plan	Right on the money
Bounce a check	Make a buck	Rubber check
Bread winner	Make ends meet	Save for a rainy day
Call in a loan/note	Make or break a person	Smart money
Cheapskate	Make out a check	Spend a small fortune
Chip in	Money is no object	Take a rain check
Corner the market	Money talks	Throw money around
Cost an arm and a leg	Nickel and dime to death	Waste not, want not
Do business with	Panhandler	

Sayings

A penny saved is a penny earned.

A fool and his money are soon parted.

The buck stops here.

He's laughing all the way to the bank.

Money is the root of all evil.

Money doesn't grow on trees.

Make/lose/spend money had over fist

Put your money where your mouth is.

QUESTION FOR DISCUSSION OR HOMEWORK

1. How does the banking system work in your country?

2. How does a checking system work in the United States?

3. (Essay question) Is it easier to use electronic payment for your bills or a checking account?

   Defend your position.

4. What is a savings account?

   Do you have one?

5. What is an IRA?

   Do you have one?   Why or why not.

6. What does "a fool and his money are soon parted" mean to you?

BIRTH CONTROL/CONTRACEPTION

Nouns/Methods

Abortion	Diaphragm	Oral contraceptives	Tubal ligation
Abstinence	Emergency contraceptive pill	Prophylactic	Vaginal lotions
Birth control pill	Foam	Rubber	Vasectomy
Cervical cap	Hormone injection	Self-control method	Withdrawal
Condom	Insert	Spermicides	
Contraceptive implant	IUD-intrauterine device	Suppository	
Contraceptive creams	Jelly	The Pill	
Day-after pill	Just say no	The rhythm method	

People

Abortion counselor	Family-planning specialist	Obstetrician
Adoption counselor	Fertility specialist	
Counselor	Gynecologist	
Doctor	Infertility specialist	

Verbs

Abort	Plan
Conceive	Say no
Have sex	Use birth control
Impregnate	

Idioms and Organizations

Abortion	Planned Parenthood	Right-to-life
Abortion clinic	Population bomb	Roe vs. Wade
Abortion rights	Population growth	Ultrasound test
Anti-abortion	Pro-choice	Women's right
Family planning	Pro-life	Zero population growth
Free choice	Reproductive rights	
Babe in the woods	Run in the family	
Be in the family way	Shotgun wedding	
It's a boy/girl	Sleep like a baby	
Like father, like son	Throw the baby out with the bathwater	

QUESTIONS FOR DISCUSSION OR HOMEWORK

1. Is birth control popular in your country?

   What type is the most popular?

2. Does the government sponsor birth control?

3. Does the government limit the number of children you can have?

   How do they do this?

4. What size family do you/would you like to have?

5. Do you believe that the government should control birth control?

6. Should there be birth control for men besides the condom?

BUSINESS AND OFFICE

Office Equipment

Adding machine
Blind carbon copy/bcc
Calculator
Computer: Hard drive
           Hardware
           Mainframe
           Network
           Personal
           Program
           Software
Conference room
Copier
Carbon copy/cc
Cubicle
Desk
Desk chair

Disc storage
Duplicate
Envelope
Equipment
FAX machine
File boxes
File cabinets
File drawers
Files
Information backup
Intercom system
Mail
Modem
Paper clip
Pencil sharpener
Postage meter

Postage scale
Printer
Records
Shredder
Stapler
Stationery
Supplies
Supply room
Switchboard
Swivel chair
Telephone
Telephone answering machine
Tape dispenser
Word processor
Work station
Voice mail

Nouns

Account
Accounting software
Accounts payable
Accounts receivable
Advertisement
Advertising/ad
Annual report
Appointment
Assets
Audit
Balance
Balance sheet
Benefits
Benefits package
Bid
Bill
Bill of lading
Bond

Debit
Deduction
Department
Department meeting
Depletion
Depreciation
Dun and Bradstreet
Equity
Estimate
Excise tax
Expenditure
Expense
Expense account
Fee
Financial statement
Fiscal year
Fringe benefit
Income

Merger
Mortgage
Negotiations
Offer
Operations
Overhead
Payroll
Petty cash
Profit
Purchase order
R & D
Receipt
Rent
Rental
Research and development
Retained earnings
Sales
Sales tax

Books
Bottom line
Business
Business card
Business meeting
Buy out
Capital
Cash flow
Commercial
Commission
Common stock
Computer
Computer support
Conference
Contract
Corporate officer
Corporate seal
Corporate secretary
Cost benefit analysis
Cost of sale
Credit
Credit check

Securities
Share (stock)
Interest
Inventory
Investment
Invoice
Labor
Labor contract
Lease
Ledger
Letter
Letterhead
Leverage
Liability
License
Labor union
Loss
Maintenance
Management
Margin
Market
Meeting

Social security
Spread sheet
Stock
Stock exchange
Stock market
Supplies
Takeover
Tax
Vale added tax
Wage
Wage scale
Worksheet
Write off

People/Personnel

Accountant	Consultant	Partner
Administrative assistant	CPA	Part-time employee
Agent	Dealer	Personnel officer
Analyst	Director	President
Assistant	Employee	Proprietor
Board of Directors	Employer	Receptionist
Bookkeeper	Executive	Salesman/woman
Boss	Executive secretary	Stockholder
Broker	Foreman	Supervisor
Bursar	Human relations/HR	Supplier
Certified public accountant	Investor	Temporary worker/temp
Chairman of the board	Lawyer	Trader
Chief	Legal counsel	Treasurer
Chief Executive Officer /CEO	Manager	Trustee
Chief Financial Officer/CFO	Office manager	Typist
Clerk	Officer	Vice president/VP
Communications specialist	Operator	Worker
Comptroller	Owner	

Type of Company

Agency	Holding company	Non-profit
Chain	Industry	Partnership
Company	Limited/Ltd.	Private
Commercial	Incorporated/Inc.	Public
Conglomerate	Monopoly	Service
Corporation	Non-commercial	Trust
Dealership	NGO	
Franchise	Non-governmental organization	

Verbs

Answer	File	Manage
Balance	Fill in	Merge
Bargain	Fill out	Negotiate
Borrow	Finance	Output
Buy	Input	Review
Collate	Invest	Sell
Copy	Lease	Staple
Design	Lend	Tender an offer
Draw	Liquidate	Transmit
Email	Loan	Type
Evaluate	Mail	Write
Fax		

Idioms and Expressions

Bullish	In the black
Business is business	In the red
Called on the carpet	Industrial wasteland
Corporate greed	Laid off
Downsized	Make a living
Earn a living	Monkey business
Employee relations	Office politics
Family business	Profit motive
Fortune 500	The bottom line
Funny business	Wage slave
Good morale	What do you do for a living?
Good reputation	Whistle blower

QUESTION FOR ORAL DISCUSSION OR HOMEWORK

1. What kind of job did you have in your home country?

2. What kind of education did you need for your job?

3. What job do you have here?

   What qualifications do you need?

4. What type of company do you work for?

5. What type of benefits do you have for workers in your country?

   Do you have benefits here?

COLLECTIVE NOUNS

People

Band	Crowd	Mob
Bunch	Family	Posse
Cast	Gang	Squad
Company	Group	Team
Corps	Horde	Troupe
Crew		

Animals

Herd Of	Flock Of	Miscellaneous Birds	
Antelope	Birds	Aerie of Eagles, hawks	Murder of crows
Boar	Chickens	Bevy of doves, swans, quail	Muster of Peacocks
Buffalo	Cormorants	Brood of Chicks, Chickens	Nest of Pheasants
Cattle	Ducks	Brood of hens	Parliament of Owls
Chamois	Pigeons	Charm of goldfinches	Peep of Chickens
Chinchillas	Sheep	Charm of hummingbirds	Rookery of Penguins (Chicks)
Cows	Turkeys	Colony of Penguins	Scold of Jays
Deer		Colony of Vultures	Sedge of Cranes
Donkeys		Company of parrots	Wake of Buzzards
Elephants		Cote of doves	Watch of Nightingales
Elk		Covey of grouse, partridges	
Gnus		Descent of woodpeckers	
Horses		Exaltation of Larks	
Moose		Gaggle of geese	
Pigs		Herd of Swans	
Yaks		Mob of Emus	
Zebras			

Fish

Bed of clams, oysters	Shoal of Fish, Salmon, Herrings
Pod of Whales, Porpoises, Dolphins	Smack of Jellyfish
School of fish, sharks	Swarm of Eels

Miscellaneous Animals

Ambush of Tigers
Array of Hedgehogs
Band of Gorillas
Bevy of Otter
Brace of Bucks
Business of Ferrets
Clan of Hyenas
Colony of Badgers
Colony of Beavers
Colony of Rabbits, hares
Colony/ Pod of Seals, Walruses
Dray of Squirrels
Drove of Donkeys

Flock of Camels
Herd/tribe of goats
Herd of Kangaroos
Herd of Llamas, Alpaca, Horses
Herd/Crash of Hippopotami
Horde of Gerbils, Hamsters
Horde of Mice, Rats
Leap of Leopards
Litter of kittens, Puppies, Cubs
Nest of Rabbits, Hares
Pack of Hounds, Dogs
Pack of Mules
Pack of Polar Bears

Pack of Wolves, Weasels
Passel of Possum
Pride of Lions
Rookery of Seals
Sleuth of Bears
String of Ponies, Horses
Team of Cattle, Oxen, Horses
Tribe of Baboons, Monkeys
Troop of Lions
Warren of Hares, Rabbits
Wing of Dragons
Zeal of Zebras

Reptiles

Army of frogs
Bale of Turtles
Bed/Den of Snakes
Float of Crocodiles
Knot of Toads

Lounge of Lizards
Nest of Vipers
Pit of vipers
Quiver of cobras
Rhumba of Rattlesnakes

Insects

Army of Ants
Army of Caterpillars
Cloud/Swarm of Gnats
Colony of Ants
Hive of Bees

Nest of Hornets
Rabble/Swarm of Butterflies
Swarm of Bees
Swarm of Flies

QUESTIONS FOR ORAL DISCUSSION OR HOMEWORK

1. Does your native language have collective nouns?

   How do you use these nouns?

2. Which of the above collective nouns have you heard used before?

   Are there any collective nouns that sound funny to you?

   Which ones?

3. Please give four (4) examples of collective nouns in your language translated into English.

CRIME AND POLICE

Police Types

C.I.A.	Investigator	Riot police
Chief of police	Meter maid	Sergeant
Constable	Narcotics office	Sheriff
Cop	Narcotics officer	State trooper
Cop	Patrolman	SWAT team
D.E.A.	Plainclothes police	Traffic cop
Deputy	Policeman/policewoman	U.S.Marshall
Detective	Prison guard	Undercover cop
F.B.I.	Private eye	Vice squad
Game warden	Private investigator	Warden

Criminals

Arsonist	Gang	Mob	Robber
Burglar	Hitman	Mobster	Serial killer
Call girl	Hood	Mole	Street walker
Con artist	Juvenile delinquent	Mugger	Swindler
Con man	Killer	Petty thief	Thief
Crook	Ku Klux Klan (KKK)	Pickpocket	Thug
Deadbeat dad/mom	Loan shark	Pimp	Tough
Drug pusher	Lynch mob	Prostitute	Underworld
Felon	Madam	Rapist	Vandal
Fence	Mafia	Rioter	Whore

Crimes

Armed robbery	Fraud	Prostitution	Terrorism
Arson	Gambling	Protection racket	White collar crime
Assassination	Gun running	Purse snatching	
Assault and battery	Harassment	Pushing drugs/dope	
Blackmail	Held up	Rape	
Break in	Homicide	Robbery	
Breaking and entering	Kickback	Sexual molestation	
Bribery	Kidnapping	Smuggling	
Burglary	Larceny	Speeding	
Con game	Manslaughter	Stalking	
Cooking the books	Money laundering	Statutory rape	
Drunk driving	Mugging	Stick up	
Embezzlement	Murder	Theft	
Extortion	Narcotics smuggling	Treason	
Forgery	Premeditated murder	Vandalism	

Events

Apprehension	Investigate	Round up the suspects
Arrest	Line up	Sentence
Chase	Mug shot	Serve time
Convict	Pay off	Speed trap
Frame	Raid	Traffic violation

Things

Assault weapon	Knife	Shotgun
Badge	Mace	Siren
Billy club	Manacles	Squad car
Brass knuckles	Night stick	SWAT weapons
Bullet-proof vest	Pepper spray	Walkie-talkie
Gun	Pistol	Wanted posters
Handcuffs	Revolver	
Handgun	Rifle	

Idioms

By hook or crook
Cement overshoes
Cops and robbers
Cosa Nostra
Crime boss
Crime doesn't pay
Crooked cop
Deadly weapon
Drive by shooting
Drug lord

Good cop/bad cop
Hit and run
In the name of the law
Inside job
Mafia
Organized crime
Police protection
Rub someone out
The "fuzz"
The "Godfather"

The "Mob"
The "Syndicate"
The rackets
Victimless crime
Witness protection program
Hate Crime

QUESTIONS FOR ORAL DISCUSSION OR HOMEWORK

1. Have you ever been the victim of a crime? What happened?

2. Have you ever talked with a policeman/woman?

    Why?

3. Do you watch police stories on TV?

    Which is your favorite show?

DEATH

Nouns

Ashes	Euphemism	Memorial service	Widow
Autopsy	Euthanasia	Mercy killing	Widower
Body	Final words	Moaning	
Burial	Funeral	Monument	
Cadaver	Funeral director	Morgue	
Casket	Funeral home	Mortician	
Catacomb	Funeral parlor	Mortuary	
Cemetery	Funeral procession	Mourner	
Cemetery plot	Grave	Mourning	
Churchyard	Grave digger	Murder	
Coffin	Graveside	Necropolis	
Coroner	Gravestone	Obituary	
Corpse	Graveyard	Ossuary	
Cremation	Headstone	Pall bearer	
Crypt	Hospice care	Sepulcher	
Death	Inscription	The dead	
Deceased	Lamentation	The remains	
Demise	Last rites	Tomb	
Dissection	Last words	Undertaker	
Elegy	Mausoleum	Urn	
Epitaph	Medical examiner	Vault	
Eulogy	Memorial contribution	Wake	

Verbs

Bereave	Eulogize	Pass on
Bury	Grieve	
Cremate	Inter	
Cry	Mourn	
Die	Pass away	

Idioms

Ashes to ashes, dust to dust

Cash in one's chips

Cause of death

Deader than a doornail

Dearly departed

R.I.P.

Give up the ghost

Deep mourning

Irish wake

Kick the basket

Open-casket funeral

Closed-casket funeral

Living will

Right to die

Wake the dead

Push up daisies

Bite the dust

Croak

Meet one's maker

Breathe one's last

Depart this life

Next life

QUESTIONS FOR ORAL DISCUSSION OR HOMEWORK

1. What are the funeral practices in your native country or religion?

2. Do you have a meal before or after the funeral ceremony?

3. Is burial in the ground common?

   Do you use a casket?

4. Do you have days of mourning?

   How many days of mourning do you have?

5. May the widowed person remarry?

   How long do the children mourn?

DENTISTRY

Office

Clinic	Office	Waiting Room
Receptionist	Billing Department	Appointment desk

Types of Dentists

Endodontics	Pediatric Dentistry
General Dentistry	Periodontics
Oral Pathology	Prostdontics
Oral Surgery	Public Health Dentistry
Orthodontics	

Equipment

Air compressor	Dentist's chair
Cleaning tools	Drill
Dental floss	Mirror
Toothpaste	Bite plate
Toothbrush	X-ray machine

Verbs

Ache	Hurt	X-ray
Cap	Inject	Clench
Clean	Pull out	
Drill	Repair	
Extract	Scrape	
Fill	Seal	
Grind	Sew	

Nouns

Abscess	Checkup	Gap toothed	Root
Baby teeth	Crown	Gum Disease	Root canal
Bicuspid	Decay	Incisor	Wisdom tooth
Braces	Dentures	Jaw	Xylocaine
Bridge	Dog tooth	Molar	
Buck teeth	Eye tooth	Nerve	
Canines	False teeth	Novacaine	
Cap	Filing	Pain	
Cavity	Front tooth	Permanent teeth	

Idioms

Baby teeth

Tooth fairy

Bite is worse than his bark

Bite the hand that feeds you

Bite off more than one can chew

Cut one's teeth one

Give an eye tooth for

Knock your teeth out

Like pulling teeth with out anesthesia

Toothy grin

Lies through his teeth

Sink your teeth into

Winning smile

Put the bite on someone

Take a bite out of something

Once bitten twice shy

Be armed to the teeth

Fight tooth and nail

Grit your teeth

Gnash your teeth

Grind your teeth

Have a sweet tooth for

Set your teeth on edge

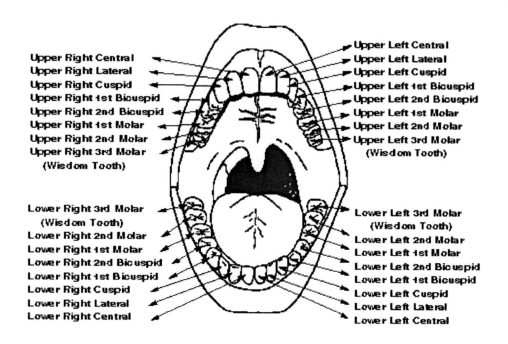

Upper Right Central
Upper Right Lateral
Upper Right Cuspid
Upper Right 1st Bicuspid
Upper Right 2nd Bicuspid
Upper Right 1st Molar
Upper Right 2nd Molar
Upper Right 3rd Molar
(Wisdom Tooth)

Upper Left Central
Upper Left Lateral
Upper Left Cuspid
Upper Left 1st Bicuspid
Upper Left 2nd Bicuspid
Upper Left 1st Molar
Upper Left 2nd Molar
Upper Left 3rd Molar
(Wisdom Tooth)

Lower Right 3rd Molar
(Wisdom Tooth)
Lower Right 2nd Molar
Lower Right 1st Molar
Lower Right 2nd Bicuspid
Lower Right 1st Bicuspid
Lower Right Cuspid
Lower Right Lateral
Lower Right Central

Lower Left 3rd Molar
(Wisdom Tooth)
Lower Left 2nd Molar
Lower Left 1st Molar
Lower Left 2nd Bicuspid
Lower Left 1st Bicuspid
Lower Left Cuspid
Lower Left Lateral
Lower Left Central

DIVORCE AND SEPARATION

Nouns

Action	Dismissal	Lump sum alimony
Affidavit	Divided custody	Marital assets
Agreement	Divorce decree	Marital property
Alimony	Documents	Mediation
Allegation	Family court	Negotiations
Annulment	Family law	No-fault divorce
Argument	Filing	Non-custodial parent
Arrearage	Filing fee	Objection
Arrears	Hearsay	Scheduling order
Assets	Joint custody	Separate property
Attorney	Joint petitioners	Separation
Best interest	Judge	Settlement
Child custody	Judgment	Sole custody
Child support	Jurisdiction	Spousal support
Collection	Legal separation	Stalker
Common law marriage	Legal custody	Standing order
Community property	On the record	Subpoena
Contested case	On-going support	Temporary alimony
Counseling	Parenting plan	Temporary support
Custodial parent	Paternity	Transcript
Custody plan	Permanent alimony	Trial
Deposition	Petitioner	Uncontested divorce
Final decree	Physical custody	Under oath
Final order	Pleading	Visitation
Fixed visitation	Postnuptial	Visitation plan
Grounds for divorce	Premarital assets	
Guardian	Retainer	
Hearing	Retainer agreement	

Verbs

Act	Divide assets	Object
Advise	Divorce	Petition
Agree	Divorced from	Plead
Allege	File	Seek custody
Amend	File for	Sell
Annul	File for	Separate
Appeal	Hear	Split up
Argue	Hide assets	Stalk
Ask for	In arrears	Subpoena
Collect	Judge	Transcribe
Counsel	Meditate	Try
Dismiss	Negotiate	Uncontested

Adjectives

Angry	Disconnected	Insensitive	Split-up
Back-stabbing	Ex-husband	Outraged	Untrue
Betrayal	Ex-wife	Puzzled	
Bitter	Faithless	Separate	
Broken	Hurt	Sorrowful	

Idioms

Broken dream, broken lives
Give s.o. the old heave-ho
Take him to the cleaners
Part company
On the brink of divorce
Be a tower/pillar of strength
Fall out of love
Come from a broken home
Marriage is about love, divorce is about money (Anonymous)

QUESTIONS FOR ORAL DISCUSSION OR HOMEWORK

1. Is divorce allowed in your country?

   Who may file for divorce?

2. Are there divorce lawyers?

   Do they cost a lot of money?

3. Who generally gets custody of the children?

4. Is there alimony for the woman if she has not worked?

EDUCATION: UNIVERSITY

Types of Colleges

4 year college	Junior college
Business school	Law school
Community college	Medical school
Dental school	Training school
Divinity school	University
Graduate school	Vocational school

Personnel

Admissions committee	Dorm director	Tutor
Associate professor	Instructor	
Chaplain	Librarian	
Coach	Professor	
Counselor	Psychologist	
Dean	Research assistant	
Department chair	Resident hall assistant	
Department head	Teaching assistant	

Places on Campus

Administration building	Dining hall	Medical clinic
Assembly hall	Dormitory	Museum
Book store	Field house	Off-campus housing
Cafeteria	Fraternity house	Playing fields
Campus police	Housing office	Sorority house
Chapel	Language laboratory	Sports stadium
Class buildings	Lecture hall	Student union
Class room	Library	Swimming pool
Computer center	Locker room	Theater

Office of

Academic dean
Academic departments
Accounting
Admissions
Alumni
Athletic department
Bursar
Campus activities

Campus dean
Chancellor
Counseling
Dean
Foreign student affairs
Health
Housing
Physical education

Registrar
Student activities
Treasurer
Tuition
University president

Degrees

BA= Bachelor of Arts
BS= Bachelor of Science
MA= Master of Arts
MBA= Masters of Business Administration
MS= Master of Science
PhD= Doctor of Philosophy

Campus Activities

Alumni reunion
Away game
Championship games
Class registration
Convocation
Examination
Faculty meeting

Final exams week
Fraternity/sorority pledge
Fraternity/sorority rush
Freshman orientation
Graduation
Hell week
Home game

Homecoming week
Kegger
Open house
Party
Prom
Vacation

Academics

ACT exams
Comprehensive exams
Continuing education seminar
Course of study
Discussion
ESL class
Field work
Final exams
Grades
Graduate Record Exams
GRE exams
Graduate school

Lab
Law boards
Lecture
Major
MCAT exams
Minor
Oral exams
Prerequisite
Quiz
Research paper
SAT exams
Schedule

Scholastic Aptitude Test
Semester abroad
Seminar
Specialty
Standardized test
Study abroad
Term paper
Thesis
TOEFL test
TOEIC test
Workshop

Nouns

"Greek" like
Academia
Academic credit
Academic freedom
Alumni group
Campus
Campus newspaper
Homecoming court
Campus radio station
Cheerleader
Co-education

Deadline
Demonstration
Diploma
Disciplinary action
Grades
Graduate
Grind
Student
Homecoming queen
Liberal arts
Literary magazine

Mortar board (hat)
Pension
Plagiarism
Post-doctoral
School magazine
Semester
Social life
Undergraduate
Year book

Idioms

Burn the midnight oil
Campus protests
Cram for exams
Hit the books
Make the grade
Politically correct campus
Receive your sheepskin
Graduate with a double major

QUESTIONS FOR ORAL DISCUSSION OR HOMEWORK

1. How does one get accepted into university in your country?

2. How does one pay for university education in your country?

3. Are there entrance exams or national exams for the university?

   Explain.

4. What did you study at university?

   How many years did it take you to get your degree?

GIFTS FOR EVENTS

Birthstones

January – garnet	July – ruby/star ruby
February – amethyst	August – peridot/ sardonyx
March – aquamarine	September - sapphire
April – diamond	October – opal/ tourmaline
May – emerald	November - topaz
June – Pearl/ moonstone	December – turquoise/ zircon

Seasonal Flowers

January – carnation	July - daisy
February- potted bulbs- hyacinth	August - rose
Paper-white narcissus	September - gladiolus
March – daffodil	October - aster
April – tulip	November - chrysanthemum
May – lily of the valley	December – poinsettia/ Christmas cactus
June – peony	Easter – Easter lily

Wedding Anniversary Gifts

1st paper	13th lace
2nd cotton	14th ivory
3rd leather	15th crystal
4th linen	20th china
5th wood	25th silver
6th iron	30th pearl
7th wool	35th jade
8th bronze	40th ruby
9th pottery	45th sapphire
10th tin	50th gold
11th steel	55th emerald
12th silk	60th diamond

QUESTIONS FOR ORAL DISCUSSION OR HOMEWORK:

1. What are traditional wedding gifts in your home culture?

2. Do you give wedding anniversary gifts in your home culture?

3. What is a traditional wedding anniversary gift in your home culture?

4. What kind of flowers would you give a person for a date?

   A gift?

   A birthday?

5. What would you give for a birthday gift in your home culture?

   In the USA?

6. Would you give a gift for a religious ceremony?

   School graduation?

   Birth of a baby?

GOVERNMENT AND POLITICS

People

Aide
Assemblyperson
Attorney General
Candidate
City Council person
Congressperson
Delegate
Governor
Incumbent
Lieutenant governor

Lobbyist
Mayor
Member of Congress
Political columnist
Political commentator
Politician
Pollster
President
Representative
Secretary of State

Senator
Sheriff
Speaker of the House
Vice President
Voter

Nouns

Apportionment
Bill
Blue state
Cabinet
Campaign
Capitol
Chancellor
Communist
Congress
Congressional district
Congressional Hearing
Congressional Record
Conservative
Democrat
District
Dogma
Election
Evolutionism
Extreme

Fascist
Hearing
House
Inauguration
Independent
Internal Revenue Service/IRS
Investigation
Legislation
Liberal
Libertarian
Lobby group
Majority
Minority
Moderate
Multi-cultural
Negotiations
Parliament
Party line
Pentagon

Petition
Political Action Committee
PAC
Polling place
President
Precinct
Prime Minister
Primary
Red state
Republican
Senate
Senator
Socialist
Special interest group
State House
Tariff
Voter registration list
Ward
White House

Adjectives

Cheat	Extremist	Libertarian
City	Fascist	Local
Compassionate	Federal	Middle-of-the road
Conservative	Honest	Moderate
County	Judicial	National
Democratic	Legislative	Republican
Dogmatic	Liar	State
Executive	Liberal	Town

Verbs

Campaign	Propose
Choose	Protest
Debate	Re-elect
Enact	Reform
Filibuster	Run for
Govern	Select
Impeach	Swear in
Influence	Take office
Lobby	Veto
Pass	Vote against
Preside over	Vote for

Issues

Abortion	Evolution	Terrorism
Affirmative action	Gay marriage	The environment
Balanced Budget	Gay rights	United Nations
Campaign contributions	Imports and Exports	War
Civil rights	Internet security	
Creationism	National security	
Discrimination	Privacy rights	
Education	Special interest groups	
Energy issues	Social Security	
Equal rights	Taxes	

Idioms and Expressions

Concede the election
Fight a losing battle
Fiscal responsibility
Grass-roots level
Honest politician
Lame-duck
Military expenditures
Minority representation
One person, one vote
Pork barrel politics
Press the flesh
Rights and obligations
Sound bite
Special interests
Take office
The military-industrial complex
Toe the party line
Undue political influence
Politicians make strange bedfellows
That government is best which governs least

QUESTIONS FOR ORAL DISCUSSION OR HOMEWORK

1. What type of government exists in your home country?

   In the USA?

2. How does one register to vote?

   Are you registered to vote?

3. How often are elections held in your home country?

   In the USA?

4. Do people want to vote in your home country?

   In the USA?

HETERONYMS

Heteronyms are a type of homograph. They are words that are spelled the same but differ in meaning and pronunciation. All heteronyms are also homographs, but not all homographs are heteronyms. Many heteronyms are similar in meaning (especially a related noun and verb are spelled the same but pronounced differently. In two-syllable English words, the noun is often stressed on the first syllable, while the verb is often stressed on the second syllable.

Here is a list of some of the most common heteronyms in the English language:

1. **Affect** - *(ah-FECT)* to change; *(AF-fect)* feeling or emotion

2. **Alternate** - *(ALT-er-nit)* another choice; *(ALT-er-NAIT)* switch back and forth

3. **Appropriate** - *(ap-PROPE-ri-ATE)* to take possession of; *(ap-PROPE-ri-it)* suitable

4. **Are** - *(AIR)* 100 square meters (a hundredth of a hectare); *(AHR)* plural present tense of "to be"

5. **Arithmetic** - *(a-RITH-me-tic)* a branch of mathematics; *(AIR-ith-MET-ic)* characteristic of arithmetic

6. **Attribute** - *(at-TRIB-ute)* to ascribe; *(AT-trib-ute)* characteristic

7. **Axes** - *(AX-ez)* plural of axe; *(AX-eez)* plural of axis

8. **Bass** - *(BASE)* a stringed instrument; *(BASS)* a fish

9. **Bow** - *(rhymes with "how")* to incline the head in greeting; also, front of a ship; *(rhymes with "tow")* weapon that shooting arrows

10. **Bowed** - *(rhymes with "how'd")* inclined the head in greeting; *(rhymes with "towed")* bent

11. **Buffet** - *(BUF-fet)* to hit; *(buf-FAY, boof-FAY)* a meal at which guests serve themselves from dishes on display

12. **Close** - *(CLOZE)* to shut; *(CLOHSS)* nearby

13. **Combine** - *(COM-bine)* threshing machine; *(com-BINE)* put together

14. **Conduct** - *(CON-duct)* behavior; *(con-DUCT)* to direct or manage

15. **Conflict** - *(CON-flict)* disagreement or fight; *(con-FLICT)* to be in opposition

16. **Console** - *(CON-sole)* upright case; also, computer terminal; *(con-SOLE)* to comfort

17. **Consort** - *(CON-sort)* companion or partner; *(con-SORT)* to keep company

18. **Construct** - *(CON-struct)* something constructed; *(con-STRUCT)* to assemble

19. **Content** - *(CON-tent)* substantive part; *(con-TENT)* satisfied

20. **Contest** - *(CON-test)* competition; *(con-TEST)* to dispute

21. **Contract** - *(CON-tract)* agreement; *(con-TRACT)* to shrink or to agree on a project

22. **Convert** - *(CON-vert)* one whose belief was changed; *(con-VERT)* to change one's belief

23. **Converse** - *(CON-verse)* opposite; *(con-VERSE)* to talk

24. **Convict** - *(CON-vict)* prisoner; *(con-VICT)* to find guilty

25. **Crooked** - *(CROOKED)* bended; *(CROOK-ed)* bent

26. **Deliberate** - *(de-LIB-er-ate)* carefully considered; *(de-lib-er-ATE)* to consider

27. **Desert** - *(DES-ert)* arid region; *(de-SERT)* to leave; also, something deserved

28. **Digest** - *(DIE-jest)* collection of published material; *(die-JEST)* absorb nutrients

29. **Do** - *(DOO)* to accomplish; *(DOE)* musical note

30. **Does** - *(DUZ)* performs; *(DOZE)* multiple one female deer

31. **Dove** - *(rhymes with "love")* a bird; *(rhymes with "hove")* jumped off

32. **Drawer** - *(DROR)* compartment that is opened by pulling out; *(DRAW-er)* one who draws

33. **Ellipses** - *(ee-LIP-sez)* plural of ellipse; *(ee-LIP-seez)* plural of ellipsis

34. **Entrance** - *(EN-trance)* entry way; *(en-TRANCE)* to captivate

35. **Evening** - *(EVE-ning)* the time of day between afternoon and night; *(EVE-en-ing)* making even

36. **Excuse** - *(EX-cuze)* to let someone off; *(ex-KYEWSS)* justifying explanation

37. **House** - *(HOWSS)* building that serves as living quarters; *(HOWZ)* to provide with living quarters

38. **Incense** - *(IN-cense)* substance that produces a pleasant aroma when burned; *(in-CENSE)* to anger

39. **Intern** - *(IN-tern)* a worker in training; *(in-TERN)* confine to a prescribed area

40. **Invalid** - *(IN-val-id)* someone who is sick or disabled; *(in-VAL-id)* not valid

41. **Laminate** - *(LAM-in-it)* a layered construct; *(LAM-in-ATE)* to construct by layering

42. **Lather** - *(hard "th")* foam or suds; *(soft "th")* one who installs lath (lattice)

43. **Lead** - *(LEED)* to guide; *(LED)* a metallic element

44. **Minute** - *(MIN-it)* sixty seconds; *(my-NOOT)* tiny

45. **Moderate** - *(MOD-er-it)* not excessive or extreme; *(mod-er-ATE)* to preside over

46. **Mow** - *(rhymes with "cow")* pile of hay stored in a barn; *(rhymes with "tow")* to cut grass

47. **Multiply** - *(MULT-i-PLY)* to perform the mathematical operation of multiplication on; *(MULT-i-plee)* in a multiple manner

48. **Number** - *(NUM-ber)* a discrete value or quantity; *(NUM-mer)* more numb

49. **Nun** - *(NUN)* women in a religious order; *(NOON)* the fourteenth letter of the Hebrew alphabet

50. **Object** - *(OB-ject)* thing; *(ob-JECT)* to protest

51. **Overhead** - *(OVE-er-head)* operating expenses; also, an overhead projector; *(ov-er-HEAD)* high; above the level of the head

52. **Pasty** - *(PAY-stee)* like glue; *(PASS-tee)* meat pie

53. **Pate** - *(PATE)* top of the head; *(PAT)* porcelain paste; *(pa-TAY)* a minced food

54. **Perfect** - *(PER-fect)* flawless; *(per-FECT)* to make flawless

55. **Periodic** - *(PEER-ee-ODD-ic)* occasional; *(PURE-eye-ODD-ic)* an iodine compound

56. **Permit** - *(PER-mit)* document giving permission; *(per-MIT)* to allow

57. **Present** - *(PREZ-ent)* gift; *(pre-ZENT)* to introduce

58. **Primer** - *(PRIHM-er)* elementary book; *(PRY-mer)* undercoat of paint

59. **Produce** - *(PRO-duce)* vegetables; *(pro-DUCE)* bring forth

60. **Project** - *(PRO-ject)* task; *(pro-JECT)* to forecast; also, to show a movie

61. **Protest** - *(PRO-test)* an objection; *(pro-TEST)* to object

62. **Pussy** - *(PUHS-ee)* having pus; *(POOH-see)* kitten

63. **Raven** - *(RAY-ven)* a black bird; *(RAV-en)* hungry

64. **Rebel** - *(REB-el)* one who refuses allegiance or opposes *(re-BEL)* to refuse allegiance or oppose

65. **Record** - *(REC-ord)* a documented account; *(re-CORD)* to set down to preserve

66. **Recreation** - *(REC-ree-A-shun)* entertaining or relaxing pastime; *(REE-cree-A-shun)* something that is remade, recreated

67. **Refuse** - *(REF-yoos)* garbage; *(ref-YOOZ)* to deny

68. **Relay** - *(REE-lay)* a race in which members of a team take turns racing; *(ree-LAY)* to lay again; *(rih-LAY)* to pass along

69. **Repeat** - *(RE-peat)* repeated television show; *(re-PEAT)* to perform again

70. **Rerun** - *(RE-run)* repeated television show; *(re-RUN)* to run again

71. **Resign** - *(re-ZINE)* to quit; *(re-SIGN)* to sign again

72. **Resume** - *(ree-ZOOM)* to restart; *(REH-zoom-ay)* document of professional experience

73. **Row** - *(rhymes with "cow")* a fight; *(rhymes with "tow")* a series of objects; also, to propel a boat with oars

74. **Sake** - *(SAKE)* purpose; *(SAH-kee)* alcoholic drink

75. **Secreted** - *(SEE-cret-ed)* placed out of sight; *(see-CREET-ed)* emitted

76. **Separate** - *(SEP-ar-ATE)* to set apart; *(SEP-ret)* not joined together

77. **Sewer** - *(SOE-wer)* one who sews; *(SOO-wer)* channel for human waste

78. **Slough** - *(rhymes with "tough")* outer layer or covering that is shed; *(rhymes with "cow")* a hole filled with deep mud or mire; *(rhymes with "through")* a marsh

79. **Sow** - *(rhymes with "cow")* a pig; *(rhymes with "tow")* to plant seed

80. **Subject** - *(SUB-ject)* the theme; also, one ruled by another; *(sub-JECT)* to force upon

81. **Suspect** - *(SUS-pect)* one suspected of a crime; *(sus-PECT)* to have suspicion

82. **Tear** - *(TARE)* to rip; *(TEER)* a drop of the clear liquid emitted by the eye

83. **Unionized** - *(YOON-yon-ized)* belonging to a union; *(un-I-on-ize)* not converted into ions

84. **Wind** - *(rhymes with "find")* to coil up; *(WINNED)* moving air

85. **Wound** - *(WOOND)* to injure; *(WOWND)* coiled up

HISTORY

Time Periods

A.D.	Century	Iron Age
Anno Domino	Common era	Millennium
B.C.	Decade	Milestone
BCE	Eon	Period
Before Christ	Episode	Pre-history
Before the common era	Epoch	Stone Age
Bronze Age	Era	Time
C.E.	Geological time	World history

People

Admiral	Frontiersman	Queen
Adventurer	General	Rabble rouser
Advisor	Geographer	Rajah
Alchemist	Hero	Ranee
Anthropologist	High priest	Rebel
Archaeologist	Historian	Representative
Artist	Indentured servant	Senator
Assassin	Innovator	Saint
Bishop	Judge	Scholar
Builder	King	Scout
Businessman	Knight	Secret agent
Caesar	Labor leader	Seer
Caliph	Leader	Serf
Captive	Merchant	Slave
Cardinal	Orator	Soldier
Chief	Paleontologist	Spy
Common man	Peasant	Statesman
Conqueror	Peon	Teacher
Counselor	Philosopher	Terrorist
Creative	Political boss	Trader
Dictator	Politician	Tradesman
Duke	Pope	Traitor
Earl	President	Tycoon
Emperor	Prime minister	Tsar
Engineer	Prince	Usurper
Explorer	Princess	Warlord
Founder	Prophet	Warrior

Historical Events

Assassination	Discovery	Inflation	World War
Battle	Downfall	Invention	
Breakthrough	Election	Massacre	
Civil war	Epidemic	Natural disaster	
Collapse	Ethnic cleansing	Nuclear explosion	
Coronation	Exploration	Overthrow	
Coup d'etat	Famine	Pandemic	
Defeat	Genocide	Plague	
Depression	Holocaust	Rebellion	

Miscellaneous

Acropolis	Genocide	Patriarch
Agreement	Gentry	Matrilineal
Alliance	Glasnost	Pax Romana
Anarchy	Global economy	Pharaoh
Apartheid	Government	Philosophy
Aqueduct	Great Leap Forward	Plebian
Aristocracy	Guild	Plebiscite
Armada	Guru	Pogroms
Armistice	Hajji	Polytheistic
Assimilation	Heresy	Predestination
Atrocity	Hieroglyphics	Primogeniture
Autocracy	Historical research	Propaganda
Balance of power	Human rights	Protectorate
Bamboo curtain	Humanist	Purdah
Barter	Imam	Purge
Bazaar	Imperialism	Radical
Biography	Impressionism	Radiocarbon dating
Blitzkrieg	Indirect rule	Rationalism
Boyars	Infidel	Reactionary
Buffer state	Infitada	Red Guard
Bushido	Inquisition	Reformation
Canon law	Internet	Reign of terror
Caste system	Iron curtain	Renaissance
Checks and balances	Isolationism	Republic
Chivalry	Jihad	Revolution
Chronicle	Judicial branch	Rhetoric
City-states	Kaiser	Ritual

Civilization	Kamikaze	Sacrament
Cold war	Karma	Saga
Collective	Legion	Samurai
Colony	Laissez-faire	Sanskrit
Communism	Latitude	Scholasticism
Conscription	Legislative branch	Scientific method
Conservatism	Liberal	Shogunate
Conservative	Lineage	Slavery
Constitution	Longitude	Social unrest
Consul	Marathon	Social upheaval
Counter-Reformation	Mastabas	Socialist
Covenant	Matrilineal	Socratic method
Crusade	Middle Ages	Sphere of influence
Democracy	Middle Passage	Starvation
Detent	Mob	Suffrage
Developing nation	Mobilize	Sultan
Dharma	Moderate	Surrender
Domain	Monarchy	Theology
Domino theory	Monk	Theocracy
Draft	Monotheistic	Tithe
Drug cartel	Mosque	Total war
Dynasty	Mullah	Totalitarian
Eastern civilization	Multinational state	Treaty
Economic growth	Nationalism	Trench warfare
Emancipation	Natural rights	Tribune
Enemy	Neanderthals	Tyrant
Ethnic cleansing	Neolithic	Tzar/tsar
Excommunicate	Nirvana	Ultimatum
Executive branch	Nomadic	Utopia
Fascism	Oligarchy	Utopian
Federal government	Oracle	Veto
Feminism	Ostracism	Viet Cong
Final solution	Pact	War
Feudalism	Pagan	Western civilization

Idioms/Expressions

...And the rest is history

A war of words

Be on the warpath

History is a chronicle of events

History is yesterday's news

Power corrupts but absolute power corrupts absolutely

Since the dawn of time

Someone is history

The history of England is the history of progress

The sands of time

This great dust heap called history

Those who do not learn from history are doomed to repeat it

War of the worlds

QUESTIONS FOR ORAL DISCUSSION OR HOMEWORK

1. When you were in school, did you have to study the history of your country?

   Of the world?

2. Did you/do you like to study current events?

3. Do you follow the nightly news on TV?

   Internet?

   Newspapers?

   Magazines?

4. Do you know any of the history of the United States?

   What events do you know?

HOMOPHONES

Homophones Level 3

AFFECT	The students affected the classroom attitude.
EFFECT	The effect of the medicine was immediate.
ALLOWED	We allowed our son to go to the school dance.
ALOUD	I read the story aloud to my children.
AIR	We need to breathe air.
HEIR	We have one heir to our fortune.
ALTAR	The altar is in the front of the church.
ALTER	I need to alter my pants. They are too big.
ARC	The rainbow is an arc.
ARK	An ark is a large boat.
BAD	I had a bad back last week.
BADE	He bade me to go on a journey.
BARON	The baron owned several small castles.
BARREN	The land was barren after the flood.
BELL	Please ring the bell loudly.
BELLE	The young belle was only 16 years old.
BERTH	I have a berth on the cruise ship to Caracas.
BIRTH	She gave birth to twins.
BOAR	The boar gave the hunters a good chase.
BORE	The play will bore me but I will go with you.
BREAD	I like to eat Indian bread.
BRED	He bred his mare to that man's stallion.
BOWL	Please put your cereal in a bowl.
BOLL	Cotton bolls are generally white.

CACHE	She has a hidden cache of money.
CASH	I need cash for the restaurant.
CANVAS	People paint on canvas.
CANVASS	We must canvass the town to get the people to vote.

CARAT	A carat is a unit of weight for gemstones.
CARROT	This carrot is a vegetable.
KARAT	This karat is to measure the purity of gold.

CAROL	We sing carols at Christmas time.
CARREL	I have a study carrel in the library.

CAST	The play has a good cast.
CAST	Jim has a cast on his leg.
CASTE	Most ancient cultures have a caste system.

CEREAL	Cereal is another name for grain.
CEREAL	I like to eat cereal for breakfast.
SERIAL	I don't like serial television shows.

CHEWS	Bob always chews his food 50 times.
CHOOSE	Bob chooses to eat cereal for breakfast.

CHUTE	The chute at the bank's drive-thru window is broken.
SHOOT	The hunter will shoot any animal he can find.

CUE	You must applaud when the manager gives the cue.
QUEUE	Your computer print order is in the queue and you'll have to wait 1 hour.

CURRANT	I love currant juice and jam.
CURRENT	The current issue of Global Rhythms is interesting.

DAYS	I will take 20 days for my vacation to Peru.
DAZE	He was in a daze after being hit in the head.

DUAL	The car has dual cams.
DUEL	The men fought a duel over the insult.

FACTS	The facts are that you are wrong about that date in history.
FAX	I will fax the information to you in a minute.

FEAT	Saving that man from the fire was a real feat.
FEET	I have 2 left feet when I dance.
FIND	I can't find the book for class.
FINED	I was fined $150 for running the red light.
FLAIR	Sheila has a flair for decorating houses.
FLARE	The red flare sparkled in the darkness.
FRIAR	A friar is a type of monk.
FRYER	This fryer is a cooking chicken.
GATE	Please board flight 669 at Gate 7.
GATE	Please close the gate behind you.
GATE	The playoffs should be the biggest gate this year.
GAIT	He has a long gait when he walks.
GENE	Every human has a gene for hair color.
JEAN	Beth likes to wear her blue jeans everyday.
GILD	I like to gild frames for pictures.
GUILD	The guild was an early union.
GOURD	I have a gourd vine from Arizona in my garden.
GORED	The bull gored the matador.
GUESSED	He guessed the right numbers and won the lottery.
GUEST	I was a guest in my brother's home for a week.
GUISE	Guise is the formal way of saying disguise.
GUYS	Hey guys! Wait for me.
HIGHER	I want to fly my kite higher.
HIRE	The boat was for hire.
HOLE	Betty fixed the hole in her pants.
WHOLE	Jim ate the whole bag of chips.
IDLE	I like to be idle on Sundays.
IDOL	I have no idols.

LAPS	Ton swam 20 laps around the pool.
LAPSE	I had a lapse of memory regarding the accident.
LEASED	Gail leased a new car.
LEAST	Buying me dinner is the least you could do for forgetting my birthday.
LESSEN	The pain will lessen over time.
LESSON	We have 2 new lessons today.
LAY	I will lay down in the sun.
LEI	In Hawaii, you will get beautiful flower lei.
LIAR	George is such a liar. He can never tell the truth.
LYRE	A lyre is a musical instrument that was used in ancient Greece.
LIE	Washington could not tell a lie.
LYE	Lye is a strong acid.
LINKS	My gold chain bracelet has 14 links in it.
LYNX	The lynx is a beautiful but dangerous cat.
LOOT	The thieves stole the loot from the car.
LUTE	The lute was an early form of a guitar.
MAIZE	Maize is the proper name for corn
MAZE	A maze is a type of labyrinth.
MALL	Teenagers like to shop at the mall.
MAUL	Be careful or the tiger will maul you.
MANNER	She has a pleasant manner.
MANOR	The Reverend lives in the manor house.
MASSED	The crowd massed along the parade route.
MAST	He bought a new mast for the sailboat.
MEDAL	USA took 1 gold medal in the triathlon.
MEDDLE	My mother would like to meddle in my business.

MIGHT	I might go to Korea or I might go to Nepal.
MITE	The dog will get mites in the forest.
MINER	The coal miner must be careful.
MINOR	If you are under 18 years old, you are a minor.
MORNING	Every morning Hal gets up at 6:30 am.
MOURNING	Herb was in mourning after his father died.
MUSCLE	I have one muscle in my arm.
MUSSEL	A mussel is a type of bivalve.
PROFIT	A company wants to have a profit every year.
PROPHET	Nostradamus was a prophet of the future.
RAISE	I try to raise my children correctly.
RAYS	The rays of the sun give warmth.
RAZE	They will raze the building to build a new road.
SERF	A serf was a type of slave in the Middle Ages.
SURF	I like to surf in Hawaii.
SURF	The surf is very strong today.
SHEAR	We must shear the sheep.
SHEER	Her curtains are very sheer.
SHOE	I lost my shoe running in the storm.
SHOO	He has to shoo the pig out of the house.
SOLE	I need a new sole on my shoe.
SOUL	Detroit is famous for soul music.
STRAIGHT	I can draw a straight line without a ruler.
STRAIT	The strait around between the 2 islands is very dangerous.
SUEDE	Suede is a type of leather.
SWAYED	The trees swayed in the wind.
SUITE	I have a suite at the hotel.
SWEET	Candy has a sweet tooth.
TACKED	I tacked into the wind.

TACT	I hardly ever use tact when I deal with parents.
TEAR	The baby had tear-stained cheeks.
TIER	I sat in the last tier of the stadium.
TENSE	Bud was tense before the exam.
TENSE	There are many tense forms of the verb in English.
TENTS	I put up 6 tents in my yard for the party.
THAI	Thai is a language spoken in Thailand.
TIE	You must tie the string in a bow.
TIE	The game ended in a tie.
VAIN	Bob is very vain about his hair.
VANE	The weather vane is pointing North.
VEIN	The vein in your body carries blood to the heart.
VARY	Clothing sizes vary so you should try on the clothes first.
VERY	He is very smart.
WAIVE	We can waive the fine if you take a defensive driving class.
WAVE	I will wave as you leave the station. Look for me and wave back.
WEATHER	The weather is very sunny but cold today.
WHETHER	I can't tell whether or not the teacher likes me.

(THE) HUMAN BODY

External Parts

Arm	Palm	Penis	Ball
Armpit	Palm	Penis	Ball
Elbow	Thumb	Foreskin	Toe:
Head	Finger:	Testes	Big toe
Hair	Index	Testicles	Little toe
Shoulders	Middle	Anus	Ball
Neck	Ring	Leg	Toenail
Forearm	Little/pinky	Thigh	
Wrist	Fingernail	Knee	**Eye**
Fist	Stomach	Calf	Pupil
Chest	Abdomen	Shin	Iris
Breast	Waist	Ankle	Eyelash
Nipple	Hip	Foot:	Eyelid
Face	Mouth	Teeth	Cornea
Forehead	Cheek	Gums	
Eyebrow	Nose	Lips	**Facial hair**
Temple	Nostril	Chin	Beard
Ear	Bridge	Dimple	Mustache
Earlobe	Jaw		Sideburns
Eardrum	Tongue		

Major Bones

Backbone	Kneecap	Skull
Collarbone	Pelvis	Spinal column
Femur	Radius	Sternum
Fibula	Rib cage	Thigh bone
Hipbone	Ribs	Tibia
Humerus	Shoulder blade	Ulna
Jawbone	Skeleton	Vertebrae

Body Systems

Digestive system	Reproductive system	Urinary system	Respiratory system
Excretory system	Skeletal system	Muscular system	
Endocrine system	Circulatory system	Nervous system	

Insides

Appendix	Liver	Tendons	Small intestine
Arteries	Lungs	Throat	Large intestine
Bladder	Muscles	Thyroid	Carotid artery
Blood	Nerves	Tonsils	Lymph glands
Brain	Ovaries	Urethra	Adrenal Gland
Heart	Pancreas	Uterus	
Kidneys	Rectum	Vagina	
Larynx	Spleen	Veins	
Ligaments	Stomach	Windpipe	

Adjectives

Tall	Sick	Obese
Short	Robust	Heavy
Fat	Weak	Skinny
Thin	Strong	Plumb
Healthy	Athletic	Lithe
Unhealthy	Tight	Skeletal
Pregnant	Loose	
Muscular	Supple	

Verbs

Ache	Cry	Jump	Smell	Twist
Belch	Defecate	Laugh	Smile	Urinate
Bend	Digest	Leap	Snap	Weep
Bite	Eat	Menstruate	Sneeze	Wink
Blink	Fornicate	Moan	Sniffle	
Breathe	Frown	Nibble	Sob	
Burp	Gasp	Pee	Spit	
Chew	Giggle	Run	Stand	
Copulate	Grin	Scowl	Stand	
Cough	Groan	See	Swallow	
Crack	Hear	Sit	Taste	
Cramp	Hop	Skip	Titter	
Creep	Hurt	Slide	Touch	

Idioms

Head

Up to my neck in work
Turn heads
Keep your head above water
Go through my head
Off the top of my head
Can't make heads or tails of
Have a hole in your head
Have rocks in your head
Put your heads together
2 heads are better than 1
Heads over heels
Use your head
Brain dead
No-brainer
Lost my head
Make up your mind
Blow your mind
Give you a piece of my mind
Boggle your mind
Pick your brains
Brainstorm
Hole in your head
Get on my nerves

Don't waste your breath
Take my breath away
Save your breath
Catch your breath
Sour puss
Hair standing on end
Pain in the neck
Take it on the chin
Turn the other cheek
Slap in the face
Make faces
In front of your face
Blue in the face
Face the music
Keep a straight face
Fall flat on your face
Jump down your throat
Swallow your pride
Loud mouth
Let your hair down
Heads up
Over my head
Get up the nerve

Mouth

Down in the mouth
Watch your mouth
Shoot off your mouth
Hand to mouth
Put your foot in your mouth
Big mouth/blabber mouth
Makes my mouth water
Word of mouth
Leave a bad taste in your mouth
Melt in your mouth
Keep a stiff upper lip
Zip your lip
Fat lip
Sharp-tongued
Forked-tongue
Lip smacker
Pay lip service to
My lips are sealed
On the tip of my tongue
Tongue-tied
Tongue in cheek
Cat got your tongue
Slip of the tongue
Mother tongue
Skin of my teeth
Eat your words
Bite the dust
Fight tooth and nail
Grin and bear it
Have the last laugh

Eyes And Ears
I'm all ears
Ear-splitting noise
In one ear and out the other
Keep an ear to the ground
Ears are burning
Wet behind the ears
Only have eyes for you
Got my eye on you
Can't believe my eyes
Eye for an eye
Make eyes at

Nose
Pay through the nose
Turn up your nose
Nose for news
By a nose
Keep your nose clean
Nothing to sneeze at
Right under your nose
Brown nose
Have a nose for
Look down your nose at
Hold your nose
Rub your nose in it
Thumb your nose at

Feet
Toe the line
Makes your toes curl
Dead on your feet
Step on one's toes
Get your feet wet
Pulling my leg
Feet of clay
Foot the bill
Land on your feet
Think on your feet
Put your foot down
Drag your feet
Foot in the door
Cold feet
2 left feet
Not a leg to stand on
Walk all over him
Walk on air
Start off on the wrong foot

Shadow
Cast a shadow over
Beyond the shadow of a doubt
Be afraid of your own shadow

Heart
Break my heart
Be young at heart
Heart-to-heart talk
Heartache
Have a heart
Learn by heart
My heart's in my mouth
Cold-hearted/hard-hearted
Heart of stone
Eat your heart out
Set your heart on
Heart of gold
Sick at heart
My heart bleeds for
Set your heart on
Have a change of heart
Your heart goes out to
Make my flesh creep

Hands

A firm hand	Get out of hand
Bite the hand that feeds you	Hands off
Evenhanded	Dismiss out of hand
Short-handed	At my fingertips
Up in arms	Dirty your hands
Elbow room	First hand knowledge
On hand	Lend a hand
Get out of hand	Have on hand
Hands are tied	Keep your hand in
Lend me a hand	On the other hand
Give him a hand (clap/help)	Show/tip your hand
An old hand	Win hands down
Have my hands full	Finger in every pie
Wash my hands of	I'm all thumbs
Red-handed	Slip through your fingers
Rule of thumb	Green thumb
Thumbs up!	Twiddle your thumbs
Get the upper hand	

Trunk

Beat your breast	Get on the wrong side of	Cover your butt
Break your back	Split your sides	Flex your muscle
Watch your back	Turn my stomach	Get it off your chest
Stab in the back/backstab	Not have the stomach for	Thorn in my side
Turn your back on	Butterflies in my stomach	Make my flesh creep
Get off my back	Lily-livered	
Back off!	Cover your butt	
Busybody	Flex your muscle	
Chip on his shoulder	Pain in the butt	
Get the cold shoulder	Bust your butt	
Look over your shoulder	Get it off your chest	
Rub shoulders with	Thorn in my side	
Shoulder to cry on	Shoulder to shoulder	
Thorn in my side	Get it off your chest	

Skeleton

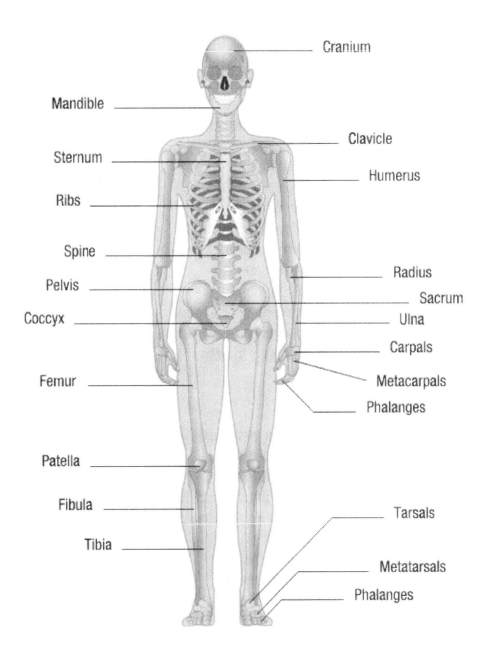

QUESTIONS FOR ORAL DISCUSSION OR HOMEWORK

1. Please describe yourself using the terms from above.

2. What verb in the list sounds funny to you?

   What verb in the list sounds interesting to you?

3. Which idioms did you know before you saw this list?

   Which ones are new to you?

4. Draw a picture showing "I'm all ears."

5. Do you ever read cartoons that use these idioms as the main topic?

   Please go on the Internet and find two cartoons.

HUMOR

Nouns

Amusement	Guffaw	Parody
Banter	Humor	Practical joke
Black humor	Humorist	Practical joker
Blue humor	Imitation	Pratfall
Burlesque	Impersonation	Pun
Caricature	Improvisation	Punch line
Cartoon	Irony	Punster
Chuckle	Jocularity	Riddle
Clown	Jocosity	Satire
Comedian	Joke	Satirist
Comedy	Joker	Sick humor
Dark humor	Kid	Sketch
Farce	Laff track	Smile
Funnies	Laugh	Spoof
Gag	Limerick	Tall tales
Gesture	Mime	Tease
Giggle	Mimic	Wit

Verbs

Amuse	Impersonate	Riddle
Banter	Improvise	Run
Chuckle	Joke	Satirize
Clown	Kid	Sketch
Guffaw	Laugh	Smile
Gesture	Mime	Spoof
Giggle	Mimic	Tease
Humor	Parody	

Adjectives

Ape	Humorless	Personal
Biting	Humorous	Sick
Blue	Ironic	Sly
Dry	Jocular	Stand up
Farcical	Loony	Uproarious
Funny	Mimic	Weird
Gut-busting	Off beat	Witty
Hilarious	Off the wall	Wry

Idioms

A good sense of humor	LOL (laughing out loud)
April Fools Day/joke	No sense of humor
Crack a joke	Pull a practical joke
Funny bone	Side-splitting
Ha-ha	Slip of the tongue
In a good humor	Tickle my funny bone
Kid around with	Tongue twister
Knee slapping	Very funny!
Laugh and a half	What a hoot!
Tell a dirty joke	Get the joke

QUESTIONS FOR ORAL DISCUSSION OR HOMEWORK

1. In your native culture, is a sense of humor prized?

2. Do you think you have a good sense of humor?

3. In you language, do you have word plays or puns?

   Do you think puns are funny?

4. Is political satire allowed in your home country newspapers?

   On TV?

   On radio?

5. What makes you laugh?

6. When you laugh in your culture, do people open their mouths and show their tongues; make loud guffaws or do they laugh quietly with mouths closed and mild laughs?

JOBS

Accountant	Exterminator	News reporter	Tree surgeon
Advertising agent	Factory worker	Nurse	Truck driver
Architect	Farmer	Ombudsman	Typesetter
Artist	Farmhand	Optician	Typist
Assembly line worker	Field hand	Optometrist	Undertaker
Automotive engineer	File clerk	(House) painter	Upholsterer
Babysitter	Firefighter	Parent	Valet
Baggage handler	Fisherman	Parking lot attendant	Veterinarian
Baker	Flight attendant	Pharmacist	Volunteer
Banker	Food handler	Photographer	Waiter/waitress
Bank teller	Garbage collector	Piano tuner	Window washer
Barber	Gardener	Pilot	Writer
Beautician	Glazier	Plumber	Zookeeper
Bookkeeper	Graphic artist	Podiatrist	"Workaholic"
Building contractor	Guard	Police officer	"Wage slave"
Beautician	Groundskeeper	Politician	
Bureaucrat	Heating contractor	Pollster	
Bus driver	Hotel clerk	Post office clerk	
Business consultant	House wife/husband	Potter	
Business man	Insurance agent	Press agent	
Business woman	Insurance claims adjustor	Printer	
Butcher	Insurance investigator	Professor	
Carpenter	Interpreter	Psychiatrist	
Car washer	Illustrator	Psychologist	
Cashier	Interior decorator	Publicist	
Chambermaid	"Jack of all trades"	Publisher	
Chef	Janitor	Receptionist	
Chiropractor	Jeweler	Real estate agent	
Civil engineer	Journalist	Repairman	
Cleaning person	Judge	Sailor	
Cobbler	Junk dealer	Sales clerk	
Con artist	Lab technician	Salesman	
Commercial artist	Landscape architect	School administrator	
Computer programmer	Laundry worker	Secretary	
Construction worker	Lawyer	Security officer	
Cook	Legislator	Shipping clerk	
Courier	Librarian	Shoemaker	

Crossing guard	Life guard	Soldier
Delivery person	Lighting contractor	Spy
Dental hygienist	Loan shark	Store clerk
Dentist	Lobbyist	Street cleaner
Detective	Logger	Student
Diplomat	Longshoreman	Surgeon
Dishwasher	Machine operator	Surveyor
Doctor	Mail carrier	Tailor
Dog walker	Maintence worker	Tax consultant
Doorman	Manager	Taxidermist
Editor	Mason	Taxi driver
Electrical engineer	Masseuse	Teacher
Electrician	Mechanic	Technician
Elevator repairman	Messenger	Telephone repairman
Employment counselor	Meter reader	Telephone operator
Engineer	Mover	Translator
Entertainer	Musician	Travel agent

QUESTIONS FOR ORAL DISCUSSION OR HOMEWORK

1. What jobs are considered "good" jobs in your home country?

   What jobs are considered "good" jobs in the USA?

2. What is your job?

   Did you have to have special training for your job?

3. Do you have "satisfaction" from your job?

   Do you like your job or is it "just a job"?

4. Do you think you are paid well or just paid enough or not paid enough?

5. What jobs to you think pay a lot of money?

6. What jobs would you like for your children?

LANGUAGE

Nouns

Adjective	Homonym	Question
Adverb	Homophone	Quotation
Antonym	Idioms	Semantics
Article	Interview	Sentence
Autograph	Jargon	Signature
Comprehension	Journalism	Slang
Conversation	Linguistics	Speech
Definition	Literature	Spiel
Dialect	Meaning	Statement
Dialogue	Monologue	Style
Diction	Narration	Synonym
Drama	Noun	Subject
Essay	Object	Syntax
Etymology	Paragraph	Theme
Exclamation	Paraphrase	Thesis
Fact	Phonology	Title
Fiction	Poetry	Usage
Grammar	Preposition	Verb
Heteronym	Punctuation	Verbiage

Punctuation

Apostrophe	Hyphen	Quotation marks
Capital letter	Parentheses	Semicolon
Colon	Period	Small letter
Dash	Period	
Exclamation mark	Question mark	

Verbs

Abridge	Drawl	Print	Sputter	Write
Call	Edit	Pronounce	Stammer	
Censor	Encode	Punctuate	Stutter	
Chat	Erase	Quote	Swear	
Communicate	Explain	Read	Symbolize	
Comprehend	Express	Recite	Talk	
Converse	Gossip	Relate	Tell	
Cry	Interpret	Report	Title	
Curse	Interview	Respond	Transcribe	
Debate	Lisp	Say	Translate	
Decode	Mean	Scrawl	Transliterate	
Define	Misspell	Sign	Type	
Delete	Mutter	Slur	Utter	
Dictate	Narrate	Speak	Vow	
Discuss	Paraphrase	Spell	Whisper	

Idioms and Expressions

Break the news

Break your word

Call a spade a spade

Call to order

Crack a joke

Double talk

Famous last words

Gobbledygook

Handwriting is on the wall

Have a way with words

Have words with

Hit the books

Hot off the presses

Keep your word

Make a long story short

Make conversation

Make small talk

Man of his word

Neither rhyme nor reason

Penny for your thoughts

Play on words

Pop the question

Read between the lines

Sign on the dotted line

Speak one's mind

Strike up a conversation

Swear on a stack of Bibles

Talk of the town

Talk to the wall

Tall story/tale

Tell it to the hand

Throw the book at

To the letter

War of words

Word for word

Word to the wise

Words of wisdom

Yackety-yak

QUESTIONS FOR ORAL DISCUSSION OR HOMEWORK

1. How many languages do you speak?

2. What part of the languages is easiest to learn?

3. Is punctuation easy to learn and use?

4. Is it difficult to be smooth and easy in a foreign language?

5. Do you think you have a way with words?

(IN THE) LIBRARY

Non-Fiction Categories

While the other categories in the library are organized alphabetically, the materials in the non-fiction category are organized according to the Dewey Decimal system.

Generalities (000-099)

Bibliography

Encyclopedia works
General collections
General organizations
General serials
Library & information sciences
Manuscripts/rare collections

Philosophy & Psychology (100-199)

Ancient/medieval oriental philosophy
Epistemology, causation, humankind
Ethics
Logic
Metaphysics
Modern western philosophy
Paranormal phenomena
Psychology
Specific philosophical schools

Religion (200-299)

Bible

Christian theology
Comparative religions
Natural theology

Social Science (300-399)

Anthropology
Commerce
Customs, etiquette, folklore
Economics
Education
General statistics
Law
Political science
Public administration
Social services
Sociology

Language (400-499)

English/Old English
Germanic languages
Greek
Italic Languages
Linguistics
Other languages
Romance languages

Natural Science & Mathematics (500-599)

Astronomy
Botanical sciences
Chemistry
Earth sciences
Life sciences
Mathematics
Paleontology/paleozoology
Physics
Zoological sciences

Technology (Applied Sciences) (600-699)

Agriculture
Building
Chemical engineering
Engineering
General technology
Home economics
Manufacturing
Medicine

The Arts (700-799)

Architecture
Drawing
Graphic arts
Landscape art
Museums
Music
Painting
Photography
Recreational/performing arts
Sculpture

Literature & Rhetoric (800-899)

American Literature
Classical
English Literature
Germanic Literature
Italic literature
Literature of other languages
Romance Languages Literature

Geography & History (900-999)

African History
Ancient History
Asian history
Biography
European History
General History
Geography and travel
North/South American History
World History

Fiction Categories

Adventure	Fantasy	Humor	Occult
Chick Lit	Feminist	Juvenile	Romance
Confession	Gay & Lesbian	Literary	Science Fiction
Contemporary	Gothic	Mainstream	Short Story
Crime	Gothic Romance	Military & War	Suspense
Erotica	Historical	Multicultural	Westerns
Ethnic	Historical Romance	Mystery	
Experimental	Horror	New Age	

QUESTIONS FOR ORAL DISCUSSION OR HOMEWORK

1. Do you ever use your local library?

2. Why do you go to the library?

3. What kinds of books do you like to read?

4. Do your children like the library and use it ?

LUCK, MAGIC AND SUPERSTITIONS

Nouns

Abracadabra	Good luck	Sorcery
Amulet	Guardian angel	Sorcerer
Angel	Heaven	Sorceress
Astral projection	Hell	Specter
Bad luck	Hellfire	Spell
Banshee	Hex	Spirit
Bat	Hocus-pocus	Spiritualism
Birth sign	Hoodoo	Spiritualist
Body snatcher	Horoscope	Telepathy
Charm	Horror story	Telekinesis
Curse	Jinx	Warlock
Demon	Magic	Werewolf
Devil	Magician	Witch
Djinn	Mumbo-jumbo	Witchcraft
Dumb luck	No luck	Witchdoctor
Esoteric	Medium	Witch hunt
ESP	Mummy	Wizard
Evil spirit	Necromancer	Wolfman
Familiar	Phantom	Undead
Genie	Premonition	Vampire
Ghost	Séance	Voodoo
Ghoul	Shaman	Voodoo doll
Goblin	Sixth sense	Zombie

Verbs

Appall	Curse	Spelled
Bewitch	Haunt	Stick
Call	Hex	Summon
Cast	Jinx	Tell
Chant	Project	Ward off
Conjure	Protect	

SUPERSTITIONS
(A belief that some action or object is lucky or unlucky)
If you break a mirror, you will have 7 years bad luck.
Step on a crack break your mother's back.
If you spill salt, throw a pinch over your right shoulder for luck.
If a black cat crosses your path, it is bad luck.
Do not open an umbrella inside.
Do not walk under an open ladder.
If your palm itches, you will receive money.
If you drop a fork, knife or spoon, company will come.

Idioms

Lucky devil

Lucky dog

Hard luck story

Beginners luck

Be down on your luck

Luck of the draw

No such luck

Push your luck

Tough luck

Cross your fingers

Knock on wood

Cast a spell

Good luck charm

Put a hex on

What the devil?

A devil of a time

The devil made me do it

Little devil/demon

Be the devil's advocate

Magic bullet

Out-of-body experience

Bag of magic tricks

Cast a magic spell

Tell fortunes

Magic charm

Magic hat

Magic wand

Magic number

Magic word

Lucky rabbit's foot

Magic carpet ride

Evil eye

Evil spirits

Necessary evil

The lesser of two evils

Good and evil

Between the devil and the deep blue sea

Speak of the devil

Give the devil his due

Magic touch

Pact with the Devil

QUESTIONS FOR ORAL DISCUSSION OR HOMEWORK

1. What are some superstitions from your country?

2. Do you believe in magic?

    Luck?

3. Do you carry "good luck" charms or amulets?

4. What is a common "good luck" charm in your country?

    In the United States?

5. Do you believe in evil spirits?

    What types of evil spirits are there?

    How do you get rid of the evil spirits?

6. Are there any good spirits?

    How do they help you?

MARRIAGE

Nouns

Anniversary	Finances	Marriage squeeze
Apartment	Fun	Marriage stages
Arguments	Gifts	Monogamy
Baby	Goals	Newlyweds
Bi-coastal marriage	Heterogamy	Nuclear family
Bigamy	Holidays	Partner
Blues	Homogamy	Polygamy
Children	Honesty	Prenuptial contract
Chores	Honor	Respect
Communication	House	Roles
Counseling	Housewife	Romance
Discussion	Husband	Same-sex marriage
Dishonesty	Infidelity	Sense of humor
Endogamy	In-laws	Sex
Exogamy	Intercultural	Spouse
Expectations	Interfaith	Stress
Extended family	Interracial	Therapy
Family milestone	Jealousy	Together time
Family pet	License	Trophy wife
Family vacation	Loyalty	Trust
Fees	Marriage marketplace	Wife

Verbs

Aim	Earn	Play	Work
Argue	Embrace	Punish	
Barbeque	Expect	Reach a goal	
Buy	Fight	Reject	
Clean	Forget	Re-marry	
Communicate	Forgive	Rent	
Compromise	Hold cuddle	Save	
Convert	Hug	Sell	
Cook	Kiss	Separate	
Cry	Laugh	Spend	
Die	Learn	Talk	
Disappoint	Love	Travel	
Discuss	Marry	Wed	
Do chores	Party	Weep	

Adjectives* * *

Abusive	Blissful	Good	Slovenly
Affectionate	Bored	Hate	Worried
Agreeable	Calm	Jolly	Gay
Amorous	Clean	Like	Lesbian
Angry	Cuddly	Lovely	Same-sex
Annoyed	Determined	Loving	
Anxious	Disorganized	Messy	
Awful	Flustered	Neat	
Bad	Frantic	Playful	
Bewildered	Friendly	Pleased	

***See Adjectives list/Emotions list

Idioms

You're just like your mother/father.

He's a chip off the old block.

Blood is thicker than water.

She's daddy's girl.

Like father, like son.

Run in the family.

Be in the family way.

Better to marry than burn.

Love and marriage rarely mix.

S/he's the spitting image of his/her father/mother.

Bring home the bacon.

Be in the doghouse.

Marriage is hard work.

Home away from home.

Hit home.

A man's home is his castle. (Old saying)

Air your dirty laundry in public.

On the mommy track.

Mama's boy.

QUESTIONS FOR ORAL DISCUSSION OR HOMEWORK

1. What are some marriage traditions in your country?

   In the USA?

2. What is a wedding ceremony like in your country?

   In the USA?

3. How are families set up in your culture?

   Are they extended or nuclear?

4. Do you have monogamous or polygamous marriages in your culture?

5. After marriage, do women work or stay home?

MEDICINE, ILLNESS AND HEALTH

Doctors

Allergist/Allergies	D.O./Osteopathy
Anesthesiologist/Anesthesiology	Obstetrician/Pregnancy
Cardiologist/Heart	Oncologist/Cancer
Chiropractor	Ophthalmologist/Eye disease
Clinical Geneticist/Genetics	Optometrist/Vision testing and glasses
Colon and Rectal Surgeon/Colon and Intestines	Orthopedic Surgeon/Musculoskeletal surgery
Dentist/Teeth, Jaw and mouth	Orthopedist/Muscles and bones
Dermatologist/Skin	Otolaryngology/Ear, Nose, Throat
Emergency Physician/Emergency Room	Pathologist/Diseases in general
Endocrinologist/Metabolism and Glands	Pediatrician/Children and Infants
Family Practioner/Family Medicine	Physiatrist/Sports medicine
Gastroenterologist/Stomach and intestines	Plastic Surgeon/Cosmetic/ Reconstructive Surgery
General Practitioner/General Medicine/G.P.	Podiatrist/Podiatry
Gerontology/Senior Care	Psychiatrist/Psychiatry
Gynecologist/Female reproductive system	Psychologist/Psychology
Hematologist/Blood	Pulmonary Specialist/Lungs
Intern	Radiologist/x-rays
Internist/Internal Medicine	Resident
M.D./Physician	Rheumatologist/arthritis
Nephrologist/Kidneys	Thoracic Surgeon/Chest Surgeon
Neurologist/Brain and Nervous system	Urologist/Urology
Neurosurgeon	Veterinarian/Animal Husbandry

Equipment/Supplies

Adhesive tape	Gauze	Sanitary swabs	Tweezers
Bandage	Heating pad	Scalpel	Vaporizer
Band aid	Ice pack	Splint	Walker
Bedpan	Latex gloves	Stethoscope	Wheelchair
Brace	Medicine	Stitches	X-ray machine
Cane	Needle	Surgical gown/cap	CAT scan machine
Cast	Operating table	Syringe	MRI machine
Crutches	Oxygen tent	Thermometer	Dialysis machine
Elastic bandage	Q-tip	Tongue depressor	Heart-lung machine

Nouns

Admitting/check in	Orderly	Urine test
Ambulance	Out-patient	Deafness
Ambulance driver	Out-patient clinic	Eyesight
Birthing room	Patient	20/20 vision
Cafeteria	Pediatrics ward	Blood pressure
Clinic	Post-operative room	Pulse
Delivery room	Practical Nurse	Reflexes
Dietician	Pre-operative room	Cure/remedy
E.M.T./emergency medical technician	Private room	Injection/shot
Emergency room/E.R.	Registered nurse/R.N	Vaccination
HMO/health maintence organization	Semi-private room	Immunization
Intensive Care Unit/ICU	Surgery	Medical chart
Lab technician	Waiting room	Pap test
Labor room	Appointment	Cervical smear
Laboratory	Medical history	Saliva
Maternity ward	Checkup/Medical Exam	Mucus
Mental hospital/insane asylum	Symptom	Blood type
Nursing home	Diagnosis	Intravenous feeding/IV
Operating room	Blood test/Blood work	Autopsy
Licensed Nurse	Stool sample	Operation

Common Remedies

Acetaminophen	Cough syrup	Over-the counter/OTC	Throat lozenges
Antidote	Contraceptive	Pain killer	Tranquilizer
Analgesic	Decongestant	Penicillin	Vitamins
Antacid	Dose	Pill	
Antibiotic	Eardrops	The pill	
Antihistamine	Eye drops	Prescription	
Antiseptic	Ibuprofen	Sedative	
Aspirin	Laxative	Suppository	
Capsule	Ointment/balm	Tablet	

Conditions

			Common
Abortion	Handicap/disability	Rash	AIDS/HIV
Ache: ear/back/tooth	Headache/migraine	Rheumatic Fever	Alcoholism
Stomach/head	Heart attack/cardiac	Rubella	Alzheimer's
Allergy/hay fever	Heartburn/indigestion/g	Rupture	Angina
Anemia	Hemorrhage	Scarlet Fever	Appendicitis
Arteriosclerosis	Herniated	Schizophrenia	Arthritis
Asthma	High blood pressure	Scratch	Autism
Bronchitis	Hurt/pain/ache	Severe/acute/sharp	Cancer
Bruise	Hygiene	Sexually Transmitted	Cataracts
Bursitis	In bad health	Shock	Chicken pox
Burning	In good health	Sick/ill	Cholera
Catch a cold	Infection	Smallpox	Diphtheria
Chills	Inflammation	Sneeze	Encephalitis
Choke	Immunity	Sore throat	Glaucoma
Chronic pain	Influenza/flu	Sprain	Hepatitis
Coma	Injury/injured	Strep throat	Hernia
Concussion	Insomnia	Stroke	Herpes
Congestion	Itch	Syndrome	Malaria
Constipation	Kidney stones	Suffer from	Measles
Contagious	Leukemia	Swelling	Meningitis
Cough	Mental Retardation	Tuberculosis/TB	Mumps
Cramp/cramps	Miscarriage	Tumor	Shingles
Diabetes/blood sugar	Mononucleosis	Twist	Typhoid
Diarrhea	Multiple Sclerosis	Ulcer	Whooping cough
Disease	Nausea/vomit/throw up	Varicose veins	
Dizzy spells	Neurosis	Virus	
Drug Addiction	Paranoia	Well	
Epilepsy/seizure	Pass out/faint	Wheeze	
Emphysema	Pneumonia	Wound/cut	
Fever/high temperature	Polio		
Fracture/break	Problem/trouble		
Gall stones	Psychosis		

Common Illnesses

AIDS/HIV	Chicken pox	Measles
Alcoholism	Cholera	Meningitis
Alzheimer's	Diphtheria	Mumps
Angina	Encephalitis	Shingles
Appendicitis	Glaucoma	Typhoid
Arthritis	Hepatitis	Whooping cough
Autism	Hernia	
Cancer	Herpes	
Cataracts	Malaria	

Common Processes

Appendectomy	EKG	Vaccinations
Blood sample	Hysterectomy	X-ray
CAT Scan	Inoculations	Allergy test
Caesarean section	Knee replacement	
Colonoscopy	MRI Scan	
D & C	Stool sample	
Dialysis	Tonsillectomy	
Drug test	Transplant	
EEG	Urine sample	

Verbs and Expressions

Ache	Throw up	Have an allergic reaction to	Nutty as a fruitcake
Admit	Vomit	Get sick/ill	Go off the deep end
Bleed	Get bed rest	Burn oneself	A bitter pill to swallow
Cough	Drink fluids	Swallow poison	In the pink
Deliver	Change your diet	Overdose on drugs	Hooked on drugs
Diagnose	Exercise	Choke	Monkey on your back
Discharge	Take medicine	Can't breathe	A shiner
Examine	Get an injection	Break a bone	Have a black eye
Faint	Run a test	Fall/slip	A shot in the arm
Give birth	Take blood	Receive CPR	Sight for sore eyes
Hurt	Take one's temperature		Under the weather
Inject	Get well	Do the Heimlich maneuver	On the wagon
Irritate	Look after	Wear a medical alert bracelet	Skin and bones
Nurse	Take care of	Make an appointment	Catch a cold
Operate	Tend to	Check your blood pressure	Come down with
Operate on	Go to the doctor	Listen to your heart	
Pain	Get physical therapy	Examine …eyes/throat/ears	
Prescribe	Get acupuncture	Draw blood	
Recover	Be injured/hurt	Give a specimen	
Recuperate	Be in shock	Get an x-ray/MRI/CAT scan	
Relapse	Have a heart attack	Go in for observation	
Swell	Have an operation	Chain smoker	
On call	Cough up	Dead as a doornail	
Turn your head and cough			
One foot in the grave	Hard of hearing	Kick the bucket	
To croak		A new lease on life	
Give up the ghost		Take one's medicine	
Over my dead body		Dead to the world	
Over the hill		Office hours	

QUESTIONS FOR ORAL DISCUSSION OR HOMEWORK

1. Have you ever been admitted to the hospital?

   What papers did they require?

2. What procedures have you had done by a doctor?

3. Have you ever had surgery?

   What type of surgery?

   Were you outpatient or in-patient?

PERSONAL RELATIONSHIPS/STAGES OF LIFE

Stages of Life

Adolescence	Childish	Juvenile	Senior citizen
Adult	Elder	Kid	Seniority
Age	Elderly	Mature	Teenager
Aged	Grownup	Maturity	Tweener
Baby	Immature	Middle-aged	Young
Child	Infancy	Pre-teen	Youngster
Childhood	Infant	Retired	Youth

People

Acquaintance	Con artist	Gangster	Playmate
Antagonist	Coward	Girlfriend	Relative
Associate	Crony	Guest	Roommate
Best friend	Crowd	Guru	Sibling
Blind date	Date	Host/hostess	Sister
Boyfriend	Disciple	Leader	Sponsor
Brother	Enemy	Lover	Spouse
Cohort	Fiancé	Mate	Team
Colleague	Foe	Mistress	Teammate
Companion	Follower	Pal	Twin
Company	Friend	Partner	
Comrade	Gang	Partnership	

Nouns

Abhorrence	Divorce	Intimacy
Admiration	Envy	Love
Affection	Friendship	Marriage
Antagonism	Hates	Rivalry
Competition	Hatred	Sex
Cooperation	Ingrate	Teamwork

Verbs

Abhor	Distrust	Intimate
Admire	Envy	Like
Antagonize	Fool	Love
Befriend	Hate	Make love
Compete	Have sex	Share
Cooperate	Ignore	Trust

Adjectives

Aloof	Dumb	Jealous	Sane
Artistic	Finicky	Kind	Self-conscious
Attractive	Foolish	Kind-hearted	Selfish
Bashful	Fresh	Lazy	Sensitive
Beautiful	Friendly	Loud	Sentimental
Bold	Gawky	Lovable	Serious
Brave	Gentle	Lovely	Sexy
Brazen	Good-looking	Mature	Shy
Cheerful	Gorgeous	Mean	Snobbish
Cold	Greedy	Mean-hearted	Spiteful
Cold- hearted	Gullible	Nuts	Stand-offish
Complacent	Handsome	Petty	Stressed out
Conceited	Hard-working	Picky	Strong
Cooperative	Helpful	Plain	Stuck-up
Courageous	Humorous	Pleasant	Studious
Courteous	Ill-mannered	Polite	Stupid
Cowardly	Impolite	Pretty	Tense
Crazy	Infantile	Quick	Trustful
Cruel	Ingratiating	Quiet	Trustworthy
Cute	Inhumane	Reliable	Ugly
Dependable	Injured	Reserved	Up-tight
Determined	Innate	Romantic	
Diligent	Insane	Rude	
Disciplined	Intelligent	Ruthless	

QUESTIONS FOR ORAL DISCUSSION OR HOMEWORK

1. What stage of life are you in?

2. Whom do you admire?

3. Whom do you abhor?

4. Whom have you befriended?

5. Whom do you love?

6. Find five (5) adjectives to describe yourself.

7. Find five (5) adjectives to describe your best friend.

PREFIXES

Prefix	Meaning	Examples
A-	Without, opposite	Atonality, asexuality, amoral, anarchy, anonymous
An (a)-	Out of	Anachronism
Ante-	Before	Antebellum
Anti-	Against	Antidote, antibody, anticlockwise
Auto-	Self	Autonomy, autobiography, automobile, autopilot
Be-	Completely, excessively; forms transitive verbs	Bemuse, bespeak, bewail
Bi-	Two	Bicycle, bicameralism
Bio-	Life	Biology, biography, biopsy
Cat/cata/cath	Down, with	Category, catalogue, catheter
Cent/centi	Hundred or hundredth	Centenarian, centimeter, centipede
Chrom-	Color	Chromatic, chromosome
Chrono-	Time	Chronology, chronic, chronicle
Circum-	Around	Circumcision, circumlocution, circumference
Co-	Together	Cooperative, co-belligerence
Con-	With, together	Connotation, Congress, congregation
Contra/con	Against, opposite	Contradiction, contraception, controversy,
Counter-	Against, opposite	Counterpoint, Counter-Reformation
Crypt (o)-	Hidden	Cryptography, cryptogram
De-	Taking something away, the opposite	Decentralization, dehydration,
deca/deka	Ten	Decahedral, December, decimeter
Deci-	One tenth	Deciliter
Demo-	People	Demographics, democracy
Derma-	Skin	Dermatology, dermatitis
Di/dif/dis	Two, double, apart, separate, opposite, not	Diurnal, divide, differ,
dia-	through	diameter, diagnosis, diarrhea
dis-	apart, separation, reverse, opposite	dissent, discovery, disambiguation
eco-	environment	economy, ecology, ecosystem,
ex-	former	ex-wife, ex-president
extra-	beyond	extraordinary, extramarital
Hemo-	Blood	Hemophilia, homophobia
Hetero-	Different, the opposite of something	Heterogeneous, heterosexual

Homo-	Same	Homogenous, homosexual
Hydro-	Water	Hydrogen,
Hyper-	Excessive	Hyperactive, hyperthyroidism
Hypo-	Below	Hypodermic, hypnosis
In-	Intensively	Inflammable, invaluable
In/il/im/ir	Not	Infallibility, illiteracy, immoral, irrelevant
In/im/il-	In, into	Instead, import,
Inter-	Between, among	Intervention, international, internet
Intra-	Inside	Intramural, intravenous, intraocular
Intro-	Into	Introspection
Kilo-	Thousand	Kilogram, kilowatt
Macro-	Large systems	Macrobiology, macroscopic
Mal-	Bad, badly	Malpractice, malnutrition
Mega-	Million, very large	Megabyte, megaphone, megalopolis
Meta-	Beyond the ordinary	Metacarpal, metaphysics
Micro-	One millionth, very small	Microgram, microorganism,
Mid-	In the middle of	Mid-term elections, Mid-Autumn Festival
Milli-	Thousandth	Milligram, milliliter
Mini-	Small	Miniskirt, miniseries
Mis-	Bad, wrong	Miscarriage, misanthropy, misogyny, mistake
Mono-	One, single	Monolith, monorail, monotony, monocle
Multi-	Many	Multiculturalism, multilingual
Non-	Not	Nonsense, nonviolence
Ob/co/of/op	Toward, against, in the way of	Obtain, occur, offer, oppose
Out-	More, to a greater degree	Outdo, outrun
Over-	More than normal, too much	Overpopulation, over-consumption
Para-	Beside	Paradox, paragon
Pent (a)-	Five	Pentagon, pentagram
Physio-	Nature, living things	Physiognomy, physiology
Post-	After, later than	Postmodernism, postindustrial
Pre-	Before	Prediction, preview, precedent, prenatal care
Pro-	For, in favor of	Pro-choice, protagonist
Pseudo-	False, not real	Pseudonym
Psych-	Mind, mental	Psychology, psychosomatic
Re-	Again, repeatedly	Reduction, reflection, revolution
Retro-	Backward	Retrograde, retrospective
Semi-	Half, partial	Semi-automatic, semi-detached
Sub/suc/suf/	Below, less than, under, beneath,	Subset, subsonic, subway, succeed,

sup/sur/sus	near	subtitles, support
Super-	Extremely, more than, over, above	Superhuman, Superego, supersonic
Syn/sym-	Together, united, at the same time	Synergy, synchronicity, synthetic
Tele-	Distance, distant	Telecommunications, television, telephoto lens,
Theo-	God	Theology, theoretical
Trans-	Across, beyond	Transfer, transubstantiation, transatlantic, Trans-Siberian railway
Tri-	Three	Triangle, tricolor, triptych
Ultra-	Extremely, beyond certain limit	Ultranationalist, ultraviolet
Un⁻	Not, opposite, take something away	Unconstitutional, untie, unfold, uncork
Under-	Below, incompletely	Underestimate, underage, undercook
Uni-	One, single	Uniform, unification, unicycle

SUFFIXES

Suffix	Meaning	Samples
-Able	Capable, can do	Usable, notable
-Age	Noun: activity, action	Marriage, mileage
-Aholic	Wants or needs (informal)	Alcoholic, workaholic, chocoholic
-Arch	Ruler, leader	Monarch, tetrarch
-Archy	Rule, leadership, highest class	Anarchy
-Athon	Sporting event	Pentathlon, decathlon
-Cede	Murder, killing agent	Suicide, regicide
-Curacy	Rule (in the context of rule by a king, rule by the people, etc.)	Democracy, theocracy
-Cy	Expressing the quality of an adjective, state or quality	Agency, idiocy
-Dom	State or condition of	Freedom, kingdom
-Ectomy	Surgical removal of body part	Laryngectomy, vasectomy
-Ed	Past	Jumped, baked
-Ent	Quality of	Different, dependent, innocent
-Er/or	Changes verb to noun (see also -or) who does the action	Writer, collector
-Er	Comparison	Harder, higher, faster
-Ery/ary/ory	Practice of, condition, place to	Laboratory, nunnery, surgery
-Ese	From a particular place	Portuguese, Taiwanese
-Ess	Female	Actress, waitress, stewardess, priestess
-Est.	Highest degree of comparison	Cleanest, hardest
-Ful	Full of, having some or much	Hopeful, useful
-Fusion	Pour together	Transfusion, confusion, infusion
-Hood	State/condition of, a group sharing characteristics	Brotherhood
-Ible/ile/il	Like -able, for Latin origins	Incredible, terrible, visible
-Ic/ical	(Adjective) relating to something	Neurotic, technologic
-Ics	Scientific study of	Physics, Aerodynamics, Forensics
–Fy, –iffy	To become, make	Magnify, falsify, beautify
-Ing	Action of	Running, wishing
-Ion	Act or state of	Confusion, protection
-Ish	Like	Childish, foolish,
-Ism	Doctrine, act, practice, condition	Protestantism, alcoholism, Buddhism,

		southernism
-Ist	Person	Dentist, Buddhist
-Itis	Inflammation of	Appendicitis, tonsillitis
-Ity/ty	Expressing state or condition	Normality, formality, banality, majesty
-Ive	Adjective: having the nature of	Defensive, aggressive, active
-Ize or -ize	To cause, to be, to become	Materialize, idolize
-Less	Lack of	Homeless, useless
-Let	Diminutive, or denoting a relation to some part of the body	Ringlet, hamlet, anklet
-Ly	-Like, having the attributes of; In modern English, primarily changes adjectives to adverbs; also changes some nouns to adjectives and some (past-tense) verbs to adverbs	Quick(adj) →quickly(adv), state(n) → stately(adj),
-Ment	State or quality, act of doing	Excitement, placement, movement
-Oid	Resembling	Solenoid, hominoid
-Ologist	One who studies a scientific subject	Archaeologist, paleontologist
-Ology	Study, science	Biology, paleontology
-Or	Changes verb to noun (see also -er)	Actor, governor
-Ous/ious	Quality from nature, chemical element	Porous
-Phobic	Suffering from	Acrophobia, claustrophobia
-Phone	Instrument or machine relating to sound	Telephone, Dictaphone
-Scope	View; instrument for viewing and observing spaces	Microscope, telescope
-Ship	State of, rank of	Friendship, relationship,
-Some	Like	Handsome, tiresome
-Stan	Land, country	Afghanistan, Hindustan
-Tude	Particular quality	Attitude, disquietude
-Ty	Quality or state of	Liberty, majesty,
-Ward/-wards	Direction, toward	Southward, inward, outward
-Ware	Stuff, things made of a particular material	Hardware, software, freeware
-Wise	Direction	Clockwise
-Y	Like, full of, action of, diminutive	Runny, messy, noisy, sooty, Bobby, puppy

TOOLS AND SUPPLIES

Tool Names

Ax, axe	Hand saw	Plumb line	Washer
Blow torch	Ladder	Power saw	Wedge
Bolt	Ladder	Router	Wheelbarrow
Brace	Level	Sander	Wire cutters
Calipers	Mallet	Sandpaper	Wood glue
Chisel	Monkey wrench	Saw	Wrench
Clamp	Nail	Scraper	Wood screw
Drill	Nut	Screwdriver	Machine screw
Drill bit	Paint brush	Square	Phillips screwdriver
Electrical wire	Paint pan	Staple gun	
Extension cord	Paint roller	Straight edge	
Flashlight	Philips screwdriver	Tape measure	
Fuses	Picture hanger	Tin snips	
Hack saw	Plane	Toolbox	
Hammer	Pliers	Vise	

Nouns

Apprentice	Construction manager	Laminate wood	Shovel
Bulldozer	Electric outlets	Pipes	Welder
Can of paint	Electrician	Plumber	Hard wood
Carpenter	Foreman	Plywood	
Construction	Helper	Primer	

Verbs

Build	Mud	Saw	Varnish
Clamp	Nail	Scrape	Weld
Construct	Paint	Screw	Wire
Cut	Plane	Shellac	
Float	Pound	Solder	
Glue	Prime	Staple	
Hammer	Put up	Tape	
Install	Renovate	Tighten	
Measure	Sand	Turn	

Idioms

Add-on to the house
Behind closed doors
Bury the hatchet
Climb the ladder
Go through the roof
Hammer home
Handyman
Hard as nails
Have a screw loose

Have an axe to grind
Hit a brick wall
Hit the nail on the head
Interesting as watching paint dry
Jack of all trades, master of none
Like a ton of bricks
Live wire
Many irons in the fire
Measure up to

Nuts and bolts
Nuts and bolts of something
On the level
Open the door for
Paint someone into a corner
Put the screws to someone
Renovate the house
Shout from the rooftops
Tighten the screws

QUESTIONS FOR ORAL DISCUSSION OR HOMEWORK

1. Have you ever built anything using more than basic tools?

2. What tools do you have at home?

3. Would you rather renovate a home by yourself or hire help?

4. Have you ever painted a room in your house?

5. Do you ever watch "DYI" shows on TV or the computer?

WEGINGS

Nouns

Accessories	Date	Invitations	Rice	Wife
Aisle	Desserts	Jewelry	Ring bearer	Wine
Anniversary	Disc Jockey	Limousine	Rites	
Bachelor	Engagement ring	Love	Services	
Bachelor party	Entrée	Maid of honor	Shower	
Bachelorette	Favors	Marriage license	Speech	
Bachelorette party	Fiancée	Matron of honor	Spouse	
Band	Fiancé	Meal	Stag party	
Banquet room	First dance	Menu	Superstitions	
Bar	Florist	Music	Sweet table	
Best man	Flower girl	Newlyweds	Tables	
Birdseed	Flowers	Pastor	Thank you cards	
Black tie	Food stations	Photographer	Thank you gifts	
Bouquet	Friends	Place cards	Toast	
Bridal shower	Garter	Prayers	Tradition	
Bride	Gift registry	Preacher	Tuxedo	
Bridesmaids	Gifts	Prenuptial agreement	Usher	
Bridesmaids gowns	Groom	Priest	Veil	
Budget	Groomsmen	Procession	Vendors	
Buffet	Guest list	Rabbi	Vows	
Caterer	Hall	Reception	Wedding album	
Champagne	Honeymoon	Reception line	Wedding cake	
Connubial	Host	Rehearsal dinner	Wedding gown	
Cummerbund	Hostess	Relatives	Wedding rings	
Customs	Hotel	Religion	Wedding video	
Dance	Husband	Religious	White tie	

Adjectives

Beautiful	Handsome	Radiant
Black	Happy	Romantic
Bliss	High-energy	Sit-down
Blue	Humorous	Small
Blushing	Joy	Sparkle
Borrowed	Large	Tasteful
Buffet	Lavish	Tasty
Delicate	Low-keyed	Unique
Delicious	New	White
Elegant	Old	Wonderful

Verbs

Accessorize	Elope	Register
Arrange	Exchange	Rent
Bake	Fit	Reserve
Book	Get engaged	Sample
Budget	Give away	Set a date
Cater	Greet	Set up
Choose	Kiss	Sewed
Constructed	Look at	Symbolize
Cook	Mail out	Taste
Coordinate	Make a toast	Throw
Cry	Marry	Tie-the-knot
Dance	Order	Try on
Decorate	Pick	Vow
Drink	Walk	
Eat	Plan	Wed

Idioms

June Bride

Blushing bride

You may kiss the Bride

Hear wedding bells

The honeymoon is over

Carry over the threshold

Jump the broomstick

Bride's family pays for the wedding

Something old, something new, something borrowed, something blue

Get hitched

QUESTIONS FOR ORAL DISCUSSION OR HOMEWORK

1. How is a traditional wedding conducted in your native culture?

   Who pays for the wedding?

   Is there a party for the wedding?

2. How does a bride dress for the wedding?

   How does the groom dress?

   The parents?

3. What was your wedding like?

   Do you have photos from your wedding?

4. What is the traditional age for marriage?

   What is the age nowadays?

   How old were you when you got married?

CPSIA information can be obtained at www.ICGtesting.com
Printed in the USA
LVOW09s2128050314

376242LV00009B/99/P